A HISTORY OF
THE BARRICADE

A HISTORY OF
THE BARRICADE

ERIC HAZAN

Translated by David Fernbach

VERSO

London • New York

INSTITUT
FRANÇAIS

This book is supported by the Institut français (Royaume-Uni) as part of the burgess Programme.
(frenchbooknews.com)

This paperback edition first published by Verso 2023
First published in English by Verso 2015
Translation © David Fernbach 2015, 2023
First published as *La barricade: Histoire d'un object révolutionnaire*
© Editions Autrement 2013

1 3 5 7 9 10 8 6 4 2

Verso
UK: 6 Meard Street, London W1F 0EG
US: 388 Atlantic Avenue, Brooklyn, NY 11217
versobooks.com

Verso is the imprint of New Left Books

ISBN-13: 978-1-78478-128-6
ISBN-13: 978-1-78478-127-9 (UK EBK)
ISBN-13: 978-1-78478-126-2 (US EBK)

British Library Cataloguing in Publication Data
A catalogue record for this book is available from the British Library

The Library of Congress Has Cataloged the Hardback Edition as Follows:

Hazan, Éric.
[Barricade. English]
A history of the barricade / Eric Hazan ; translated by David Fernbach.
pages cm
Includes index.
ISBN 978-1-78478-125-5 (hardback) – ISBN 978-1-78478-127-9 (ebook) – ISBN 978-1-78478-126-2 (ebook)
1. Insurgency–France–Paris–History. 2. Revolutions–France–Paris–History. 3. Barricades (Military science)–France–Paris–History. 4. Paris (France)–History. I. Fernbach, David, translator. II. Title.
DC719.H3913 2015
355.4'260944361–dc23
2015020817

Typeset in Fournier by Hewer Text UK Ltd, Edinburgh
Maps designed by Mélanie Marie (www.2m-cartographie.com), Paris, France
Printed and bound by CPI Group (UK) Ltd, Croydon, CR0 4YY.

Contents

'For the rest, the barricades are retrenchments that belong to the Paris spirit: they are found in all our disturbances, from Charles V to our own day.'

—Chateaubriand, *Memoirs*

Preface

That streets should be used as battlefields is an idea perhaps as old as cities themselves. And since the very first urban combats, people no doubt tried to protect themselves by piling up whatever they had to hand: planks, rubble or carts. The barricade, however, is not a regular retrenchment. A heap of disparate objects, combined in a moment, its particular virtue is to proliferate and form a network that crosses the space of the city. This faculty of rapid multiplication can make it an offensive instrument: victorious barricades, as we shall see, are those that pin down the forces of repression, paralyse their movements and end up stifling them into impotence.

The history of the barricade stretches across three centuries. It starts at the height of the Wars of Religion, quickens in the course of the nineteenth century, and ends with the Bloody Week that marked the end of the Commune. (Its extensions in the twentieth century are almost a different story.) It takes place principally in Paris: a Parisian invention, the barricade is the common point of the majority of riots, insurrections and revolutions that punctuate the history of the city and the country – with the sole exception of the French Revolution, in which its role was belated and minor. At certain points, moreover, it was copied elsewhere, as at Lyon in the 1830s or across Europe at the time of the 'springtime of the peoples' in 1848.

Writing this history has not been easy: the barricade is intermittent by nature, which makes it impossible to set down a neat linear story. What I have tried here, however, is to show a certain continuity: in this symbolic form of popular revolt we find across the centuries the same material elements, or nearly so – youngsters, stallholders, workers, students, defending their street, their district, their way of life against forces that are always superior in both numbers and weapons; and on the other side, Swiss guards in the service of kings, or peasants brought by rail from the depth of the provinces. Behind the paving-stones, rifles and flags, it is these heroes and heroines that I have tried to bring back to life from the anonymity into which official history has cast them.

We could say that this is only a succession of defeats – some immediate, on the ground, others delayed – in which the forces of domination end up reversing the gains of an ephemeral victory. But thanks to Baudelaire, Blanqui, Hugo and Lissagaray, this is a history that is still living, a source of inspiration for those unresigned to the perpetuation of the existing order.

Chapter 1

The Barriers of the League: May 1588

Barricade: the word makes its first appearance in the *Commentaires* of Blaise de Monluc, the warlord who commanded the royal troops against the Huguenots in Guyenne in the 1570s. He had a certain personal experience of it. In September 1569, he attacked Mont-de-Marsan: 'The enemies fired straight at the bridge, along a main road, where they had put a barricade, which they were not all able to reach, as we caught a large force in the side roads. . . . Finally the enemies abandoned the barricade and hastened into the other town by the gateway.' (Mont-de-Marsan had three concentric walls, and this attack was directed against the outermost of these.) When the town was taken, Monluc had the garrison executed. In July 1570 he laid siege to Rabastens, a fortified bastide on the banks of the Tarn, 'the strongest castle that was in the power of the queen of Navarre':

> I had three or four ladders brought to the edge of the ditch, and as I turned back, I was struck by an harquebusade from the corner of a barricade touching the tower: I believe there were not as many as four harquebusiers there, as all the rest of the barricade had been destroyed by two cannon firing from the flank. Suddenly I was covered in blood, flowing from my mouth, nose and eyes. . . . But wiping the blood as best I could, I said to monsieur de Goas: 'Make sure, I pray you, that no one collapses, and continue the combat.'

A surgeon, 'by the name of Simon, opened me and removed the bones of both jaws with his fingers, so great were the holes, and cut the flesh of my face, which was all crumpled.'[1] After the bastide was taken, Monluc still had the strength to order 'that not a single man escape without being killed'. It was during his convalescence that he wrote his *Commentaires*, while the leather mask was being made that he would wear until his death to hide his destroyed face.

But Guyenne was a remote place, and the war waged by Monluc against Henri de Navarre is not a major chapter of history. The official birth of the barricades dates from some twenty years later: on 12 May 1588, the regular troops that Henri III had brought into Paris were hemmed in by the tight mesh of barricades erected by the population, and narrowly escaped massacre. This famous Day of the Barricades marked both a turning point in the Wars of Religion that had ravaged France for more than twenty-five years, and the first large-scale and effective use of this tactic, fixing for a long time to come both the practical modalities of its use and its political significance.

Henri III, who had previously been king of Poland, came to the throne of France in 1574 on the death of his brother Charles IX (the king of the St Bartholomew massacre). He was not popular, particularly in Paris, which at that time was very Catholic and traditional. His entourage was lampooned, the famous 'mignons' who passed their time in duels and debauchery of various kinds. He was attacked for his fantasies, his cross-dressing, his taste for lapdogs and exotic animals. Pierre de L'Estoile, gentleman usher to the chancellery and quite royalist in his sympathies, related in his diary that on 14 July 1576:

> The king and queen arrived in Paris on return from the land of Normandy, from where they brought a large quantity of monkeys, parrots, and small dogs purchased in Dieppe. Some of these parrots, the majority trained by the Huguenots, gave out all kinds of

---

1   Blaise de Monluc, *Commentaires* (Paris: Picard, 1925), pp. 239, 344.

nonsense and railing against the mass, the pope, and the ceremonies of the Roman church; when some people who had been offended said this to the king, he replied that you don't interfere with the conscience of parrots.[2]

But there were more serious matters. Henri III had granted concessions to the Protestants such as freedom of worship and the fortification of their towns, leading people to think that he was not far from supporting their cause. Worse still, as he had no direct heir and his brother, François d'Anjou, had died in 1584, the successor to the throne had to be his closest relative, Henri de Navarre. That the crown of France might fall to a Protestant was for the Catholics, and the Parisians in particular, a vision of horror, a quite unacceptable eventuality.

Paris, as the centre of intransigent Catholicism, lost no time in organizing under the impulsion of the League. This politico-military force had been built up around the Guise family in Nancy, capital of the duchy of Lorraine. With the backing of Spain and the pope, its aim was to ensure the maintenance of the Catholic religion in France, and to root out Protestantism. Its leader was Henri de Guise, *le Balafré* or 'Scarface'. In Paris, the League carried out propaganda work and prepared for a confrontation that people felt to be close. The duke and his Paris emissaries had divided the city into five parts, each headed by a colonel and four captains, all experienced fighters. The priests preached openly against the king and his entourage, and weapons were stockpiled at the Hôtel de Guise.[3]

Informed by his spies, the king decided to bring things to a head. He forbade the duc de Guise to come to Paris, 'and if he should come,

2 Pierre de L'Estoile, *Journal de L'Estoile sur le règne d'Henri III* (Paris: Club des Libraires de France, 1963), p. 62.

3 This stood on the site of the present Hôtel de Soubise, which houses the Archives Nationales. The two towers overhanging the rue des Archives are vestiges of it.

matters being in the state that they were, a disturbance could be caused, in which case he would be permanently held to be the author and culprit of any evils that should arise'.[4] On 9 May, the duke defied this order and made his entry, surrounded only by eight gentlemen. A vast crowd acclaimed him as he passed, crying: 'Long live de Guise! Long live the pillar of the Church!' 'A young lady at a stall even lowered his mask and said aloud these words: "Good prince, since you are here we are all saved." ' He proceeded directly to the Louvre, where the king gave him a frosty reception. The duke denied any hostile intention, but he returned the next day, this time with an escort of 400 men, which was not intended to facilitate a reconciliation, despite the efforts of the queen mother, Catherine de Médicis.

Henri III had taken precautions, strengthening the guard around the Louvre and assembling a force of 2,000 French guards and 4,000 Swiss to the north of Paris, close to the Porte Saint-Denis but outside the walls. When any accommodation with the duke began to look impossible, he ordered a complete search of the city for weapons, and the arrest of infiltrators. The force needed was made up of the troops massed at the city gates, who made their entry during the night of 11–12 May 1588.

On Thursday, 12 May, the king stationed the guards companies at the Saint-Séverin crossroads and the Pont Saint-Michel, in the Marché Neuf on the Île de la Cité, on the place de Grève (now de la Concorde), in the Innocents cemetery and around the Louvre:

> He sought by this means to carry out what he had already resolved with his council, that is, to seize a number of the bourgeois of Paris, of the League, the most evident, and some partisans of the duc de Guise . . . and have all these troublemakers and rebels killed at the hands of the executioners, to serve as an example to other adherents of the duc de Guise's party.

---

4   L'Estoile, *Journal*, p. 282. The unreferenced quotations that follow are taken from this work, pp. 282–9.

It was this intrusion that triggered the Day of the Barricades:

> When we rose, the people saw this new and unaccustomed specta-
> cle; they were seized by fear, believing that this was a garrison
> designed to be placed in the city, a new occasion of servitude. Some
> who had more sense deemed that it was a preparation against
> monsieur de Guise, preventing the people from obstructing this.[5]

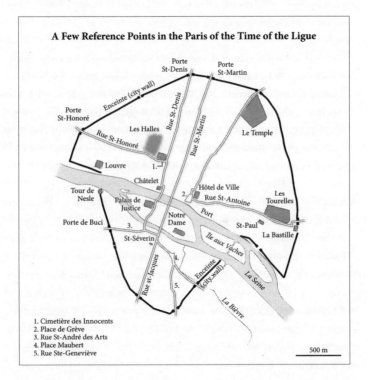

A Few Reference Points in the Paris of the Time of the Ligue

1. Cimetière des Innocents
2. Place de Grève
3. Rue St-André des Arts
4. Place Maubert
5. Rue Ste-Geneviève

500 m

5 Étienne Pasquier, *Lettres historiques pour les années 1556–1594* (Geneva: Droz, 1966), p. 290. Pasquier, like L'Estoile a direct witness, was advocate-general at the Chambre des Comptes, and a humanist who strongly condemned the St Bartholomew's Day massacre.

The city of Paris, 'where one had never seen nor heard of a foreign garrison being installed', had always enjoyed the privilege of not receiving soldiers within its walls, not having to lodge them or undergo the habitual brutalities that went with this. The entrance of the troops was an attack on this communal privilege which aroused the whole population, whether League supporters or not. So that this day was both a political insurrection by the League and a popular revolt against the introduction of soldiers into Paris. It is this double nature that explains why the city rose up en masse:

> Upon this, each person hastened to take up arms, went out on guard by streets and quarters, and in no time put chains across and made barricades at the street corners. The artisan left his tools, the merchant his wares, the university scholars their books, the prosecutors their bags, the advocates their *cornettes*, the presidents and the very councillors took up halberds. All that was heard were terrifying cries, seditious murmurs and words to inflame and frighten the people.[6]

According to tradition, the first barricades were put up in the morning around the place Maubert, following the instructions of the comte de Brissac, one of the lieutenants of the duc de Guise. According to L'Estoile: 'The bourgeois of the Saint-Séverin crossroads who were aroused and assisted by the comte de Brissac, who had already in the morning reached the side of the University, armed the students and had the first barricades made towards the rue Saint-Jacques and the quarter of the place Maubert.' By the end of the morning the Latin Quarter was covered in barricades, and, by evening, so was the whole centre of the city.

It is quite possible that Brissot was the inventor of the barricade. What at all events is certain is that the construction that made its first appearance in Paris that day no longer had anything in common with

---

6   L'Estoile, *Journal*, p. 285. The following quotations are from pp. 286, 287.

the chains that it had long since been the custom to stretch between houses to block passage. These barricades were made of upturned carts, cobblestones, pieces of furniture, and above all *barriques* (barrels), filled with earth to give them solidity. The network of these was so dense that soldiers were caught as if in a net, under fire from the barricades and neighbouring houses. One detachment that tried to reach the place Maubert from the Île de la Cité was blocked by barricades in the rue Galande. 'The Swiss guards were prevented in this way from passing and came to a halt. Following the example of this barricade, every quarter did the same to stop other soldiers in their tracks.'

Henri III, seeking to avoid bloodshed, sent marshals d'Aumont and de Biron to organize the retreat of the troops to the Louvre, which proved difficult:

> As these poor Swiss could not do much, throwing down their weapons and shouting '*Bonne France!*' and calling for mercy with their hands together, the furious people, from the Petit-Pont to the Pont Notre-Dame, almost killed them by striking with their harquebuses and other weapons, as well as the rocks and stones that women and children threw from the windows.

The following day, the king sent the maréchal de Biron to the duc de Guise to ask him to restore order in the city. The duke proceeded to the worst trouble spots and prevented a massacre of the Swiss guards. Without him, L'Estoile wrote, they would all have been dead. In Pasquier's words: 'The morning was for the king, until around ten o'clock; the rest of the day for monsieur de Guise, who, seeing himself in a strong position, mounted a horse, in his doublet [i.e. unarmoured], followed by a large company of men, promenading throughout the city, and indeed using his goodness with remarkable modesty.' The duc de Guise managed to free the Swiss guards blockaded in the slaughterhouse of the Marché Neuf, and released Le

Gast, captain of the French guards and one of the king's 'mignons', who had taken refuge in a house on the rue Saint-Jacques.

Henri III's situation, however, remained critical. The city authorities were worried:

> Now, the provost of merchants and aldermen seeing that this armed and mutinous people who had remained in tumult the whole night, arms in hand and defiant in the streets, continued again this day and threatened to do worse, supported secretly by the duc de Guise and his partisans who grew stronger by the hour and were filing into the city, they went to the Louvre accompanied by some captains of the city to speak to the king and show him that if he did not give a prompt order to pacify this tumult, his city of Paris would be lost.

Catherine de Médicis then sought a reconciliation:

> The queen mother, who throughout her dinner had not stopped weeping, set out for the Hôtel de Guise to try to calm this emotion, which was such that she could scarcely pass through the streets, being so densely strewn and retrenched with barricades, where those guarding them were reluctant to make a greater opening for her chair to pass. Finally, arriving there, she spoke to the duc de Guise, prayed him to extinguish the fires that had been lit, and to come and see the king from whom he would have as much satisfaction as he might expect, and make clear to him on such an urgent occasion that he had more desire to serve the crown than to weaken it. To which the duc de Guise, with cold mien, replied that he was very sorry, but it was not up to him, it was the people, and they were like maddened bulls and difficult to restrain. As for going to see the king, he said that to him the Louvre was strangely suspect, that it would show great feebleness of mind for him to go there, things being in a state that he deplored, and to cast himself helpless and unarmoured at the mercy of his enemies.

It is surprising that the duke did not show the same foresight at Blois, where he was murdered.

But the king, seeing the barricades dangerously close to the Louvre, decided to leave the city. 'At five in the afternoon, having received notice from one of his servants, who slipped into the Louvre in disguise, that he would have to escape more or less alone, or he would be lost, he left the Louvre on foot, a stick in his hand, as if going to walk in the Tuileries as was his custom.' He escaped on horseback by the Porte Neuve,[7] followed the Seine as far as Chaillot and Auteuil, and with a handful of loyal followers took the road for Rambouillet.

Thanks to the barricades, the popular movement and the action of the League supporters had expelled the king from Paris. The duc de Guise was master of the city. But these insurrectionary days marked the high point of the League, which would soon experience a succession of defeats – the assassination of the duc de Guise at Blois, the battles lost to the royal forces by his brother, the duc de Mayenne, the four years of the terrible siege of Paris, and finally, the entry of Henri IV into the capital on 22 March 1594, putting an end to the Wars of Religion.

---

7   The Porte Neuve was at the western corner of the Tuileries on the Seine side.

Chapter 2

The Barricades of the Fronde: August 1648

A *fronde* is a sling made from a leather pouch held by two laces, and containing a stone that is hurled by releasing one of the laces. It is the weapon with which David slew Goliath, and which children in the countryside would use to kill sparrows. By what curious detour did this little device give its name to the troubles that shook France in the late 1640s, one of their most serious moments being a second Day of Barricades, on 26 August 1648? The answer is unclear. That some youngsters used slings to break a number of windows at Mazarin's hôtel is scarcely sufficient.

What is certain is that in that year the state was shaken by a revolt of lawyers, particularly members of the Parlement of Paris. Following the authoritarian regime of Richelieu and Louis XIII, power was exercised by a regent, as Louis XIV was only five years old on the death of his father in 1643. The regent, Anne of Austria, widow of Louis XIII, was assisted by a royal council, the country's real government, in which the leading figures were Gaston d'Orléans, brother of the late king, against whom he had constantly plotted throughout his reign; Prince Henri de Condé, the father of the man who would become the 'great Condé', the chancellor, Séguier, and above all Cardinal Mazarin. The influence of the latter on the regent steadily grew, and he attracted general loathing from both princes and parlementarians, not counting the people, who despised and lampooned this Italian too accustomed to a conspicuously sumptuous lifestyle. However diverse their interests, the participants in the Fronde had at least one common goal: to get rid of Mazarin.

Early in 1648, the kingdom's finances found themselves drained by the expenses of the long war against the Habsburgs, particularly against Spain, which constantly threatened the north of France from the Netherlands. A large part of the receipts of the royal treasury depended on tax collectors called *partisans*, who would later be known as *fermiers généraux*: the royal council auctioned off, at very high prices, contracts that authorized the *partisans* to collect indirect taxes throughout the country. These *partisans* handed the proceeds to the treasury, after deducting their share. The tax farmers were hated for their arrogance, their rapacity and their style of life, but the royal council was all the more defenceless against them as they acted as bankers to the crown, advancing ever more money secured against future receipts.

The interest rates that the farmers demanded became prohibitive, and it was no longer possible to keep the treasury afloat in this way. The situation became critical when it was necessary to finance the spring military campaign, and rumour had it that the mercenaries whose wages had not been paid were refusing to march. The superintendent of finances, d'Hémery, proposed new taxes and the creation of twenty-four new posts of *maître des requêtes* – the sale of new offices would allow substantial returns.

The treasurers, however, royal officials charged with collecting direct taxes (including the feudal *taille*), seeing the people so pressed that any rise in taxes risked leading to an explosion, stopped work: we would say today that they went on strike. The seventy-two *maîtres des requêtes*, pillars of royal authority in the judicial domain, also decided to stop hearing court cases, in protest against the creation of new offices that diluted the value of those they possessed. Within a few weeks, the movement extended to all the legal personnel, the Parlement of Paris, the Grand Conseil or Great Council, the Chambre des Comptes (chamber overseeing the royal receipts and public spending) and the Cour des Aides (fiscal court). In spring 1648, the entire judicial and financial business of the kingdom came to a halt.

This movement was illegal, but the Paris parlementarians had in front of them the example of the English parliament, which had just won the civil war against Charles I, likewise provoked by the king's financial troubles. It is true that the two parliaments had nothing in common but the name. The French parlementarians, who bought their office and whose functions were solely judicial, had no legitimacy to speak in the name of the people; but the Paris parlement had come to view itself as the representative of the country in the face of the arbitrariness and incompetence of the public authorities: it judged that it had to debate the difficulties of the state.

Despite the authoritarian gestures of the regent and the royal council, and in defiance of a *lit de justice*[1] aimed at having the new taxes and creation of offices recorded as laws of the realm, the parlement and the sovereign courts held firm. Delegates from each of the chambers met in the Hôtel Saint-Louis of the Palais de Justice. On 13 May 1648, a 'decree of union' sealed this passage en bloc of all the legal personnel into opposition to the royal power:

> The Cour des Aides sent a deputation to the Chambre des Comptes, to solicit unity with it for the reform of the state. The Chambre des Comptes accepted this. Each of them were guaranteed by the Great Council, and the three together demanded the cooperation of the Parlement, which was happily granted, and executed without delay in the Palais, in the hall known as Saint-Louis.[2]

---

1 A *lit de justice* was a session of the parlement in the presence of the king. The parlementarians' role here was merely advisory, royal decisions having the force of law whatever the opposition.

2 *Memoirs of Jean François Paul de Gondi, Cardinal de Retz* (Boston: L. C. Page, 1899), book 2. At the time of the Fronde, Retz was not yet a cardinal, but

Anne of Austria's response was to imprison five treasurers and summon the parlement to the Palais-Royal.[3] But she failed to get the parlementarians to agree to return to their regular judicial role and cease meddling in government affairs. Pressed towards reconciliation by Gaston d'Orléans, the regent accepted the decree of union with bad grace.

On 30 June, the meeting at the Hôtel Saint-Louis submitted to the parlement a very bold series of articles: the intendants of the provinces, the direct representatives of royal power, were to be recalled; the *taille* would be reduced by an eighth for the year 1648, and all arrears written off; no subject of the king could be held in prison for more than twenty-four hours without being brought before a judge; the *lettre de cachet* was to be suppressed.[4] This meant the collapse of what had been for Richelieu the foundation of the state. Even the expression traditionally appended to the parlement's decrees, 'by the good pleasure of the king', was to be supplemented or replaced by 'with liberty of suffrage'.

The impasse was total, when great news arrived from the north: the army commanded by Condé (the son) had won a decisive victory over the Spanish at Lens, on 20 August. The regent believed that this event gave her an advantage: the victorious army could march on

---

co-adjustor (chief assistant) of the archbishop of Paris, under the name of Gondi. He wrote his memoirs twenty-five years after the events of the Fronde. Though he often puts himself in a favourable light, and historians have questioned some of his assertions, his verve, humour, and the beauty of his language make this text irreplaceable. [Here and in the following quotations, this 1899 translation has been modified. – *Translator*]

3   In 1643, the regent and the child king Louis XIV were established in the Palais-Cardinal bequeathed to the crown by Richelieu, which then became the Palais-Royal. Only a few vestiges remain of the building of that time, submerged in the palace built by Victor Louis in the 1780s.

4   Orest Ranum, *La Fronde* (Paris: Seuil, 1995), p. 140.

Paris and make the rebel parlementarians see reason. She decided to have those whom she viewed as the chief inciters imprisoned, and used the occasion for this of a *Te Deum* celebrated in Notre-Dame on 26 August to give thanks for the victory. The future Cardinal de Retz officiated. The regent, the boy king, the ministers and the judges of the sovereign courts attended the ceremony:

> As was the custom, all the streets were lined with soldiers of the guards regiments, from the Palais-Royal to Notre-Dame. As soon as the king had returned to the Palais-Royal, these soldiers were formed into three battalions, who remained on the Pont-Neuf and the place Dauphine. Comminges, lieutenant of the queen's guards, seized the worthy Broussel, councillor of the Grande Chambre, and took him to Saint-Germain in a closed carriage. Blancmesnil, president of the Enquêtes, was seized at the same time in his house, and taken to the Bois de Vincennes.[5]

The 'worthy Broussel', as Retz disdainfully called him, was one of the most respected parlementarians. According to Omer Talon, advocate-general of the court of Saint-Louis,

> M. de Broussel lived close to Saint-Landry, in the street known as Port-Saint-Landry [near Notre-Dame]; and since he was a former officer, aged sixty-three, giving support to the poor and with a reputation for protecting the interests of the people against the vexation of new taxes, and as for the last three months the whole city of Paris was full of hope from what had happened in the chamber of Saint-Louis and what had been decided in the parlement, in all of which actions M. de Broussel had been seen as a party leader, who had always put forward the proposals that were most advantageous to the people, as soon as his domestic servants shouted

---

5   Cardinal de Retz, *Memoirs*.

throughout the city that M. de Broussel had been arrested and taken away, the people of the city rose up, and it seems very likely that his people, learning of this disaster in their household, had insinuated into the minds of their neighbours, shopkeepers and other towns-folk that the intent was to do injury to this monsieur Broussel because he protected the interests of the people.[6]

Broussel's arrest accordingly triggered lively emotions in the quarter: 'I cannot express,' wrote Retz, 'the consternation that was visible in Paris in the first quarter of an hour after the seizure of Broussel, and the movement that arose in the second. The sadness, or rather devastation, even affected the children; people looked at one another and said nothing. Suddenly someone burst out: rise up, run, shout, close the shops.'

The tocsin began to sound, chains were stretched across the streets of the Île de la Cité, and people began to build barricades. 'I found on the Pont-Neuf,' reports Retz, 'the marshal de La Meilleraie at the head of the guards, and although there were only at that time some children who were shouting insults and throwing stones, he was overjoyed to see me, perceiving that the clouds began to thicken on all sides.'

This relief was justified. The royal guards who had remained in place after the *Te Deum* received the order to go and occupy the Palais de Justice, but their advance through the Cité was difficult, since, just like the Swiss guards sixty years before, they were bombarded with projectiles and fired on with muskets from the roof-tops. They were forced to retreat along the rue Saint-Honoré until the Palais-Royal. During this time, the city militia had assembled on the order of the provost of merchants (equivalent to the Paris mayor),

---

6 *Mémoires* of Omer Talon, in *Collection des Mémoires relatifs à l'Histoire de France, depuis l'avènement d'Henri IV jusqu'à la paix de Paris conclue en 1763* (Paris: Foucault, 1827), vol. 61, p. 244.

with the idea of restoring order. But these bourgeois militias, commanded by officers who were in many cases parlementarians, were very hostile to Mazarin. Out of opposition to the government, and also from fear of popular riot and looting, the militias worked to construct barricades in the centre of Paris on the night of 26–27 August, a night during which 'two or three persons were killed, by indiscretion rather than design', writes Talon.

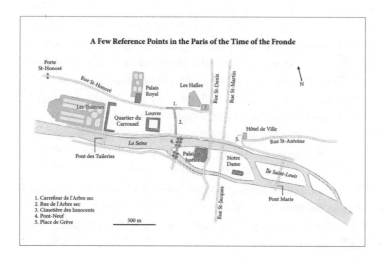

A Few Reference Points in the Paris of the Time of the Fronde

1. Carrefour de l'Arbre sec
2. Rue de l'Arbre sec
3. Cimetière des Innocents
4. Pont-Neuf
5. Place de Grève

On the morning of the 27th, the regent and Mazarin sent Chancellor Séguier 'to take his place in the parlement and explain to them the anger of the queen, and read them a decree of the [royal] council annulling everything that had been done by the parlement since last July'.[7] But the chancellor did not manage to reach the palace. The bridges were barred, he was forced to abandon his carriage, and

7   Talon, *Mémoires*, p. 250.

hemmed in on every side, [he] narrowly escaped with his life to the Hôtel d'O, which the people broke open, rushed into with fury, and, as God would have it, fell immediately to plundering, so that they forgot to force open a little chamber where both the chancellor and his brother, the bishop of Meaux, to whom he was confessing, lay concealed.

Retz's tale shows how much the memory of the events of 1548 remained alive in the popular mind.

The news of this occurrence ran like wildfire through the whole city. Men and women were immediately up in arms, and mothers even put daggers into the hands of their children. In less than two hours above two hundred barricades were erected, adorned with all the standards and colours that the League had left entire. All the cry was, 'God bless the king!' and sometimes, 'God bless the co-adjustor!' and the echo was, 'No Mazarin!'

During this time, the assembled parlement had decided to proceed 'in a body and in full formal dress' to the Palais-Royal, to demand the liberation of Broussel. Talon, who was one of the delegation, relates the course of events:

The face of the city of Paris was unrecognizable: all men, young and old, and small children from the age of twelve, had arms in their hands, shouting that they wanted M. de Broussel to be released. From the palace to the Palais-Royal we found eight barricades made by chains stretched in places where this was possible, by beams put across, by barrels filled with paving-stones, earth or rubble; besides this, the intersecting streets were also barricaded everywhere, and at each barricade a bodyguard composed of twenty-five or thirty men armed with all sort of weapons, all the townsfolk declaiming that they were at the service of the parlement, shouting '*Vive le roi! Vive le parlement! Vive M. de Broussel*', and that we had to return him.[8]

The regent decided first of all to refuse the audience, which had not been solicited in advance as protocol demanded. She then changed her mind, supposedly influenced by Queen Henrietta, daughter of Henri IV and widow of Charles I of England. This unfortunate queen pointed out to her that events had begun in the same manner on the other side of the Channel.

The delegation was headed by the first president of the parlement, Mathieu Molé – 'the most intrepid man to appear in this century', according to Retz, generally very sparing with praise. He demanded the release of the imprisoned parlementarians, insisting on 'the peril in which the public was placed by the tumultuous taking to arms'. The queen mother, 'who feared nothing because she knew little, flew into a passion and raved like a fury, saying: "I know too well that there is uproar in the city, but you parliamentarians, together with your wives and children, shall be answerable for it all"; and with that she retired into another chamber and shut the door after her with violence.'

The delegation prepared to leave, but the regent, after discussions with Séguier, Gaston d'Orléans and Mazarin, made it known that she would agree to release the prisoners, provided the parlement ceased to meet together with the other sovereign courts and returned to its customary judicial capacity.

The parlementarians felt that they could only respond to such a demand after due deliberation in their own chambers. They decided, accordingly, to go back to the palace. 'We were told', relates Talon, 'a strange thing by the domestic officers in the king's house: "Stand firm, your councillors will be returned to you"; and among the French guards, the soldiers said out loud that they would not fight

---

8   Ibid..

against the townsfolk but would lay down their arms, such was their contempt for the government.'[9]

The return of the parlementarians would not be unproblematic. The first barricades were opened to them, but when they reached the Croix du Trahoir – at the corner of the rue de l'Arbre-Sec and the rue Saint-Honoré, one of the main Paris crossroads, the insurgents (an anachronistic word, but it fits the reality) refused to let them pass, berating them for their failure to obtain the liberation of Broussel. A famous image is of one of them, a butcher (Retz calls him a *rôtisseur*), brandishing a pistol (or a knife, or a halberd, depending on the source) under Molé's nose, saying: 'Go back, traitor, and if you have a mind to save your life, bring us Broussel, or else Mazarin and the chancellor as hostages.' Certain judges, fearing not unreasonably for their lives, took refuge in houses nearby, but the intrepid Molé gathered those who remained and continued towards the Palais-Royal, where he was offered refreshment and a room in which to hold their discussion, in the presence of Gaston d'Orléans and Chancellor Séguier. Finally, the majority of judges decided to accept the regent's conditions. Armed with letters duly signed and ordering the release of the prisoners, the parlementarians left the Palais-Royal, but as Broussel was still not to be seen, the barricades remained in place during the night of 27 August:

> The entire city was in alarm and on perpetual watch, and the least noises whether accidentally heard or deliberately excited led to rumours throughout the city, greatly increased by nine or ten o'clock in the morning, at which time M. de Broussel reached Paris, being saluted by all the harquebusiers at each guard post.[10]

All along the way the crowd gave Broussel a triumphant reception, from the Porte Saint-Denis to the Île de la Cité, then 'the barricades

9   Ibid., p. 253.
10   Ibid., p. 258.

were demolished, the shops opened, and in less than two hours Paris appeared calmer than I had ever seen it on a Good Friday'.

These days were a spectacular episode at the start of the Fronde, which would continue for four years. The Fronde of the parlement was followed by the Fronde of the princes, rich in sudden events, the last of which would be the confrontation between Turenne and Condé along the eastern wall of Paris at the beginning of June 1652. The duchesse de Montpensier, 'la Grande Mademoiselle', had the city gates opened so as to enable the remnants of Condé's army to escape being crushed. Louis XIV kept a lasting grudge against Paris because of these events that he had seen as a child, always refusing to establish himself there; indeed, the construction of Versailles was one of the consequences of the Paris barricades of August 1648.

There are certainly similarities between the barricades of May 1588 and those of August 1648. They were constructed from the same elements: an upturned cart, furniture, 'beams placed across, [and] barrels filled with paving-stones'. In both cases, they were put up at a speed that amazed witnesses (an amazement that would be voiced in almost the same terms before the speed with which the students raised barricades in the rue Gay-Lussac on the night of 10 May 1968). The entire population took part in their construction, including women and children. From their starting-point – place Maubert in 1588, the Île de la Cité in 1648 – they spread in a few hours across the entire city centre. Above all, they were completely effective. The royal troops were trapped in a network of barricades built very close together – more than a thousand barricades in an area whose diameter was around one kilometre. Whether Swiss or French, the soldiers were poorly commanded by officers who quite understandably lacked the faintest idea of what an urban insurrection was. In both cases, they were reduced to a pitiful retreat under musket fire and stones thrown from buildings.

The main difference between these two events, therefore, lies in terms of politics rather than warfare. While the barricades of the

League, if not initiated by the supporters of the duc de Guise, were at least built and recuperated by them, what is striking about those of the Fronde is their spontaneous character. The thing was done without leaders: neither Broussel, nor the parlementarians, nor Retz – no matter what he claimed – were at the origin of the barricades of 1648. They neither foresaw nor directed these, nor did they even really exploit them. The barricades resulted from a movement of general indignation by the Paris population in the face of unjustified arrests, against a background of hatred towards the foreigner, Cardinal Mazarin, who sought to perpetuate the arbitrary rule of Richelieu's time.

How could an insurrection without leaders take hold of the largest city on the continent in just a few hours? Rumour, word of mouth, contagion from one neighbour to another, does not explain everything. The answer must be sought in the collective memory of the people. In August 1648, the barricades of the League were only sixty years in the past – more or less the same span that separates us today, for example, from the Mendès-France government, and everyone knows how alive the memory of that still is today. We have seen in Retz, and the same is found in several of his contemporaries, allusions to the League, and it may well be this memory that enabled the almost spontaneous generation of a general insurrection. Spontaneity, the absence of leaders and strategy, also explain why the *journées* of 26 and 27 August, spectacular as they may have been, did not have a follow-up. When Broussel returned and the barricades were taken down, Paris was 'calmer than on a Good Friday'.

From then until the end of the Ancien Régime, there would be no more barricades raised in France. If violent confrontations continued to take place, their locus was in the countryside and no longer in the big cities. In Paris, the 'great enclosure' of 1657 was conducted without obstacle, with beggars, prostitutes, blasphemers, attempted suicides and mad people being confined within the walls of the Hôpital Général (the Salpêtrière, Bicêtre, the Pitié,

Sainte-Pélagie). In the age of classicism, the very word 'barricade' seemed like a baroque vestige – making the title of François Couperin's pieces for harpsichord of 1717, the year of Watteau's *Pilgrimage to the Isle of Cythera*, all the more surprising: *Barricades mystérieuses*.

Chapter 3

The Hunger Barricades: Prairial Year III

It is often claimed that the barricade was absent from the French Revolution, and this is almost true. In Paris, the battles that led to the taking of the Bastille in July 1789 and the fall of the monarchy in August 1792 were not street fights, confrontations propitious to barricades. Elsewhere, the battles that took place at Thionville, Verdun, Lyon or Toulon were sieges in which artillery played the main role, so much so that barricades such as those Monluc encountered two hundred years before would have been as archaic as the harquebus.

It was only with the ebb of the Revolution, during the long phase of reaction that followed the elimination of the Robespierrists on 9 Thermidor year II (27 July 1794), that the barricade made its reappearance in Paris – an episode of a few hours, limited to the Faubourg Saint-Antoine, without real fighting but of great historical significance, as it marked the final uprising of those who would still for a while be known as sans-culottes.

'Bread and the 1793 constitution!' This slogan echoed by the Paris population in spring 1795 sums up the reasons for the Prairial insurrection: poverty and anger. The winter of 1794–95 had been particularly severe: the rivers had frozen and blocked the arrival of firewood. Numb with cold, but having made it through to the spring, the Parisians would now suffer hunger. The Convention in the hands of the Thermidoreans had dismantled the regulations put in place by the Montagnards early in year II, the cornerstone of which had been the 'maximum', or the fixing of a maximum price for essential goods. Prices were set by a commission of subsistence, which organized requisitions in the countryside and punished hoarding and speculation. The system was not perfect, but it staved off famine and the depreciation of paper money, the *assignat*.

In 1795, these measures were gradually abolished. The result was that peasants who had only reluctantly accepted the requisitions refused to hand over their harvests in exchange for paper, and demanded coin. Stocks collapsed, speculation grew, and the government increased the 'maximum', which had the effect of driving prices still higher and the *assignat* still lower. It was naturally the poor who suffered most from the situation. Women stood all night outside the bakeries waiting for them to open, often returning empty-handed to their famished children as the bakers had not received any flour. In these interminable queues, agitation increased: speculators and merchants were blamed, and the government said to be hand in glove with them. On 1 Germinal year III (21 March 1795) the Convention adopted a decree proposed by Sieyès against 'seditious gatherings', but it was unenforceable, since not everyone could be thrown in jail.

Besides hunger, there were political grievances. Many sans-culottes believed that the Revolution would continue after Thermidor, only without the heavy hand of the great Committee of Public Safety; but they were rapidly disillusioned. On all sides the counter-revolution triumphed. On 22 Brumaire (12 November 1794) the Jacobin Club was closed under threat of the bludgeons of the gilded youth, the so-called *muscadins*. The leader of these 'young people', as they were called, was Fréron, who had distinguished himself by his bloody exploits in the repression of Marseille and Toulon under the Montagnard Convention. On 20 Pluviôse year III (8 February 1795), the ashes of Marat were removed from the Panthéon and thrown in the sewer. On 11 Ventôse (1 March

1795), Fréron demanded the punishment of four members of the former Committee of Public Safety, the 'Decembrists' Billaud-Varenne, Collot d'Herbois, Barère and Vadier. On the 18th of the same month, the Girondins outlawed in summer 1793 were recalled to the Convention. All these measures provoked popular indignation. By demanding the constitution of 1793, what the sans-culottes wanted was the dissolution of a Convention they no longer trusted and the election of a new assembly. In the popular quarters, people were openly saying that it was time to sound the alarm and take to the streets.

On 12 Germinal (1 April 1795), troops were concentrated in the faubourgs and the Île de la Cité. Militants from the sections gathered outside the Convention, chased off the guards and irrupted into the chamber. The majority of deputies left the hall in disarray, and the Montagnards themselves,[1] far from taking the head of the movement, used it to have the Convention evacuated. Without leaders or direction, the crowd finally dispersed. The next day, an Assembly barely recovered from the fright decreed the arrest of fourteen Montagnard deputies, and the deportation of the four 'Decembrists' to Guyana.[2]

This was only a partial reprieve. A few weeks later, disturbances resumed. On 30 Floréal (19 May 1793) an anonymous pamphlet appeared, *Insurrection du Peuple pour obtenir du Pain et reconquérir ses Droits*: in it the people were enjoined to dismiss and arrest the present

---

1 Those who remained after the Thermidor purge. They were few in number, and known as the 'Crête' or Crest.

2 For a detailed account of this *journée* (and those of Prairial), see Evgenii Tarlé, *Germinal et Prairial* (Moscow: Foreign Languages Publishing House, 1959); also Kåre D. Tønnesson, *La Défaite des Sans-Culottes* (Oslo: Oslo University Presses, 1959). Billaud-Varenne and Collot d'Herbois were actually deported, Barère managed to escape, and Vadier, who had fled at the time of Germinal, remained in hiding until the amnesty voted at the end of the Convention.

government, establish immediately the constitution of 1793, and organize the election of a new legislative assembly. To accomplish this programme, the people were to proceed to the Convention en masse the next day.

Indeed, on 1 Prairial (20 May), at five in the morning, the tocsin sounded in the faubourgs Antoine and Marceau.[3] First in the popular quarters, then in the central ones, groups of women ran through the streets, burst into workshops, mobilized their sisters and urged the sections to take up arms. By the end of the morning several hundred women were marching on the Convention to the beat of drums, headed by a woman of twenty-one dressed as a man.[4] Then the battalions of the three sections of the faubourg Antoine (Popincourt, Quinze-Vingts and Montreuil) also set off for the Tuileries, leaving their commanders and officers behind. Along the way they recruited sans-culottes from the centre and east sections of Paris.

The crowd gathered at the Carrousel, entered the Tuileries and broke down the doors of the meeting hall. Deputy Féraud, who tried to resist, was killed by a pistol shot, and his head paraded at the end of a pike in the place du Carrousel. The rioters massed around the tribune, and in the commotion one of them read from the pamphlet *L'Insurrection du peuple*. As on 12 Germinal, however, nothing came of this chaos; the government committees could prepare their counter-offensive. National guards from the western sections of Paris, loyal to the Convention, evacuated the hall, and the deputies then voted the arrest of fourteen of their number, guilty of having spoken in favour of the insurrection.

The next day, 2 Prairial, the government stationed an armed force around the Tuileries, making any new invasion of the Convention impossible. The sans-culottes assembled at the Hôtel de Ville, raising

---

3   With the de-Christianization of autumn 1793, the word 'saint' had disappeared from the names of all places and streets.

4   Tønnesson, *La Défaite des Sans-Culottes*, p. 259 ff.

fears for a moment of a revival of the insurrectional Commune of August 1792 – an unpleasant memory for the Thermidoreans – but no decision was taken. The irresolution of the Prairial insurgents, their lack of clear direction, would soon be fatal to them. The following day, the government organized a real army to take control of the faubourg Antoine. This was formed by troops of the line, cavalry, carabineers, duly selected National Guard, and Fréron's 'young people' – some 20,000 men in all. 'Paris at this moment resembled an armed camp. You could not move a step without coming across some cavalry or infantry corps, all marching without being preceded by any trumpets or drums. The national garden [Palais-Royal] was full of troops, and entrance was prohibited.'[5]

On 4 Prairial (23 May), at five o'clock in the morning, a column commanded by General Kilmaine left the place du Carrousel. Kilmaine has described his expedition himself.[6] His column was made up of

> the battalion of young men, called the vanguard battalion, detach-ments from the sections of La Butte-aux-Moulins, Lepelletier and Champs-Élysées, supplemented by 200 dragoons, a total of 1,200 men, with two artillery pieces. My instructions were to proceed with this division to the faubourg Saint-Antoine, to surround Santerre's house,[7] and seek out Cambon and Thuriot who were hidden there.

---

5   'Paris, 4 prairial', *Journal des hommes libres*, 5 Prairial, quoted in Tønnesson, *La Défaite des Sans-Culottes*, p. 311.

6   Kilmaine, *Détails circonstanciés de ce qui s'est passé le 4 prairial au faubourg Saint-Antoine*, Bibliothèque Nationale, département des imprimés, Lb41, 1826, gallica.bnf.fr.

7   Santerre's house stood on the corner of the faubourg and the rue de Reuilly. A plaque at 9 rue de Reuilly recalls the memory of the former commander-in-chief of the National Guard. Cambon and Thuriot, who had both played an important role in the fall of Robespierre, were by this time seen as extremists.

The column followed the quays, the place de Grève, the rue Saint-Antoine.

> I went almost right through the faubourg, Santerre's house being at the far end. I placed the troop in battle order and had the house searched from top to bottom; during this operation, I sent patrols to find out what was happening behind me, and inform myself of what had become of the reinforcement that should immediately have followed me, but of which I had not perceived any sign.[8]

Kilmaine would easily have been able to reach the far side of the faubourg (the place du Trône-Renversé, now de la Nation), but he learned that behind him the sans-culottes of the faubourg had erected barricades to cut off his retreat. 'This exit would have had the air of a flight and of having been dictated by fear. . . . I was firmly resolved to oblige the same men who had sought to enclose us to take down their barricades themselves.'

The column therefore set out for the Bastille:

> We set out on march, accompanied by the commissioners of the Quinze-Vingts;[9] we were greeted by cries and the most atrocious insults from a multitude of armed men and a still greater number of women, or rather furies, who wanted to cut our throats, so they said; I let the cries die down, and summoned them, in the name of the law and the national representation, to hand over the killer [of Féraud] and those who had saved him from the scaffold, and to immediately open the barricade, which I threatened, in case of refusal, to demolish by cannon fire. . . . After having used threats

---

8   This had been diverted to the Pont Marie to prevent the arrival of sans-culottes from the faubourg Marceau.

9   The commissioners of sections, appointed and paid by the government, were loyal to the Convention.

and reason in turn, and particularly after the movement of our gunners to position their batteries, we managed to open a passage. We marched on and reached the second barricade, where we were met by the same cries. After a quarter of an hour we succeeded in having it opened, but the word spread that the rearguard had seized the cannon of the Montreuil section. The rebels immediately set to work to close the barricade; cries and shouts recommenced. Several people climbed up to the windows to attack us with rifle fire, which made the position of our cavalry in particular very alarming, as it was impossible for them to defend themselves in the barricaded streets against men firing on them from the first floor.

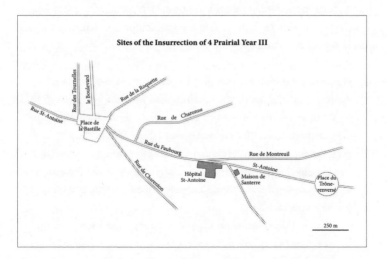

Kilmaine decided to hand back their cannon to the Montreuil sans-culottes, the barricade was opened, and the column continued its way:

When we reached the last barricade we encountered a more stubborn resistance than at the two former ones, increased by a large number of wandering citizens from the Indivisibilité section and the main rue Saint-Antoine. . . . Tired of the little success of reason, I had the cannon pointed at the barricade, resolved on rapid fire if I was not obeyed within three minutes. Finally, the column managed to reach the boulevard [Beaumarchais].

As Kilmaine explains, it might easily have been massacred, blocked as it was between the barricades and very inferior in number to the insurgents. It escaped only because the sans-culottes had no plan and no leader. Spontaneity is often a good counsellor for the offensive, but more rarely when it is a matter of defence against a force commanded by experienced officers like Kilmaine, who had fought at Valmy and Jemmapes.

At four in the afternoon, five columns left from different points to converge on the faubourg. That commanded by Kilmaine found itself on the rue Saint-Antoine:

We were obliged to fire two or three rifle volleys at men placed on the corner of the rue des Tournelles, who were insolent enough to try to disarm some men of our vanguard. . . . I told them that if in the time prescribed they had not obeyed the orders of the Convention, the faubourg would be reduced to ashes and the next day it would be as if it had not existed. . . . The result was that the cannon were surrendered. Our young men lifted the barricade and opened up the whole faubourg.

During this time, a prodigious number of armed men and women pressed towards us down the rue Saint-Antoine; I had them contained by a hundred dragoons who acted in such a way as to leave no hope to the partisans of revolt; detachments from each column entered the faubourg to cries of 'Long live the Convention, Long live liberty, Long live the republic, down with the Jacobins, down with the brigands!' The cannon were handed over, the leaders of the revolt were arrested, and we returned to the Convention showered with the blessings of an immense crowd in every street.

The redoubtable sans-culottes of the faubourg Saint-Antoine had been reduced to unconditional capitulation. After this decisive defeat, the people of Paris did not play a political role for a long time to come.

In the days that followed, a military commission condemned thirty-six insurgents to death. The same penalty was meted out to six deputies held responsible for the insurrection: Romme, Duquesnoy, Duroy, Bourbotte, Soubrany and Goujon. On hearing the sentence, each stabbed himself with a knife that was passed from one to the next, from breast to hand. Three died of their injuries, the three others were taken dying to the guillotine. Soubrany was dead on arrival, but his corpse was guillotined nonetheless.

Chapter 4

Barricades and the End of the Bourbons:
November 1827, July 1830

After a long absence, the barricade reappeared in Paris on a night in November 1827. As in Prairial year III, the event was short-lived and limited, but while the exit of the sans-culottes from the stage had marked the end of an era, this occasion saw the opening of a long history of insurrection in Paris, with wide echoes across Europe in the nineteenth century.

In 1827, under Charles X, the council of ministers headed by Villèle had succeeded in uniting against it both the liberal opposition and a section of the royalists, in protest against a press law proposed in December 1826, which Chateaubriand had termed the 'vandal law'. The withdrawal of this law, after it had been torn to pieces in the upper house, led to celebration in the popular districts. On 29 April, Charles X proceeded to the Champ-de-Mars to review the 20,000 men of the Paris National Guard. Cries of 'Long live the king!' were mingled with others that were far less acceptable: 'Freedom of the press!', 'Down with the ministers!', 'Down with the Jesuits!' 'The offended king replied: "I have come here to receive homage, not lessons." He often had in his mouth noble words that did not always support vigorous action,' wrote Chateaubriand.[1] The same evening, a

---

1 François-René de Chateaubriand, *Mémoires d'outre-tombe*, book xxviii, chapter xvi.

decree was issued dissolving the Paris National Guard – an impulsive move that would have fatal consequences for the monarchy.

As the political situation was blocked, Villèle decided to bring matters to a head. On 6 November, *Le Moniteur* published three further decrees. The first appointed seventy-six new peers, including five archbishops and forty deputies who were government supporters. The second decree abolished censorship, which had been recently imposed but was forbidden in an election period. The third dissolved the Chamber of Deputies and convened electoral colleges by arrondissement (particularly in Paris) for 17 November, and for the departments on the 24th. Faced with this effective coup d'état, which 'violently changed the composition and spirit of this Assembly [the house of peers] and . . . could not leave the slightest doubt as to the all-powerful action of the religious party', on the next day 'the newspapers of the royalist and liberal opposition published coalition lists which, for the first time since the onset of representative government in France, brought together under the common title of *constitutional candidates* politicians who had previously been of greatly opposed opinions.'[2]

'An immense current of opinion', Vaulabelle continues, 'drove all minds to a single thought, a single aim, to break the detested ministry.' In Paris, the eight opposition candidates were elected by an overwhelming majority: Benjamin Constant obtained 1,033 votes against twenty-two for his opponent, and the others won by similar margins. All the ministerial candidates were defeated in what was a real rout.

The elections took place on 17 and 18 November. The following day was calm, but in the evening the crossroads were lit up in the

---

2   Achille de Vaulabelle, *Histoire des deux Restaurations* [1844] (Paris: Perrotin, 1860), vol. 7, pp. 319–20. Vaulabelle was a moderate republican, and became minister of public instruction in 1848. His account of the days of 18–19 November is lively and precise, and perhaps that of an eye-witness, or at least a well-informed observer. The unreferenced quotations that follow are taken from pp. 319–29 of this volume.

quarter around the rues Saint-Denis and Saint-Martin (not yet divided by the boulevard de Sébastopol), attracting a crowd of passers-by whose demeanour 'showed only two sentiments, joy at the success of the opposition, and curiosity'. Some individuals, circulating among the groups, sold petards. A police commissioner sent to observe delivered a report in which the concern is apparent:

> Almost all the houses in the rues Saint-Denis, Saint-Martin, or those adjacent, are lit up. . . . Rockets and petards are being thrown on the public way; men, mainly sales clerks, are walking about with an unfurled umbrella in their hand, topped with a lighted candle. Every now and then, musket or pistol shots can be heard from within buildings; in a word . . . there is a repetition of all the scandalous scenes that took place when the law on the license of the press was withdrawn.[3]

Towards ten o'clock, while those simply curious were starting to retire, Vaulabelle writes that

> a band of fifty to sixty adolescents mostly aged from twelve to fifteen, dressed in blouses and rags, or wearing work clothes, suddenly irrupted into the crowd with cries of 'Up with the opposition deputies!', mingled with these strange slogans: '*Vive Napoléon!*', '*Vive l'empereur!*', '*Les lampions!*'[4] These new arrivals carried in their aprons or blouses stones that they hurled against the windows of houses that were without light or where the lights had been extinguished.

---

3 Cited by Anne-Marie Lauck, 'Les troubles de la rue Saint-Denis ou le renouveau des barricades à Paris le 19 et 20 novembre 1827', in Alain Corbin and Jean-Marie Mayeur, eds, *La Barricade* (Paris: Publications de la Sorbonne, 1997), p. 58. The unreferenced quotations that follow are taken from the documents reprinted in this work.

4 This call for *lampions*, or illumination, was for people to light up their houses.

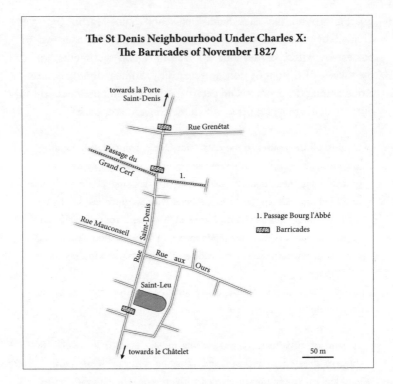

The St Denis Neighbourhood Under Charles X: The Barricades of November 1827

towards la Porte Saint-Denis

Rue Grenétat

Passage du Grand Cerf

1.

Rue Mauconseil

Rue Saint-Denis

Rue aux Ours

Rue

Saint-Leu

1. Passage Bourg l'Abbé

Barricades

towards le Châtelet   50 m

Some young people then seized hold of water-carriers' barrels and carts stationed near the Innocents market, using them to block the rue Saint-Denis:

> Houses were being demolished at a short distance from this market and the rue Grenétat [today Greneta]; poles and planks were taken from the scaffolding, stones heaped up, and new paving-stones that had been brought to repair the roadway; all these materials were placed across the public road, and new barriers were built . . .

. . . the still unformed germ of the modern barricade.

The crowd attacked the police station on the rue Mauconseil, and the expression of joy turned to confrontation.

At ten in the evening, after no police force had appeared, a detachment of gendarmes arrived from the rue Grenétat. Received with boos and stones, they pressed the crowd back into the side streets and demolished the barricades, which the young people rebuilt as soon as the gendarmes departed, 'amid laughter and shouts of encouragement from the crowd of spectators, who were amused by the sight of such novel scenes.' A little later on, reinforcements entered the rue Saint-Denis from each end, the Porte Saint-Denis and the place du Châtelet. The gendarmes of the latter detachment,

> on arriving at the second barrier and being met with stones and shouts of 'Down with the gendarmes!', were obliged to retrace their steps, first of all to the Pont au Change, and then to the prefecture of police. . . . The troop that left from the boulevards was larger, made up of gendarmes on foot and on horse; it came all the way down the street, demolished and cleared all the barricades amid a hail of stones, and halted at the Innocents market, where it took up position.

As the situation had become serious, the prefect had royal guards and troops of the line assemble on the place du Châtelet. Divided into three columns and headed by police commissioners, these made their way up the rue Saint-Denis. One of these columns arrived at the Grand-Cerf barricade where it was met with stones:

> Its head, Captain Bouvier, did not take the time to read the summons; he ordered his men to fire; a concentrated fire was directed at the barricade and the houses closest to it; the soldiers then marched on the barricade; it was abandoned and destroyed. That of Saint-Leu offered still less resistance. . . . At the same time as the troop was tackling these two obstacles from the front, squads of gendarmes on foot and on horse spread into the neighbouring

streets, charging with sabres or bayonets at all the individuals they could reach. A few hours later, the morgue received several corpses, and the hospitals a number of workers who were mortally wounded or seriously injured.

In the rue aux Ours, a young student by the name of Auguste Blanqui was struck by a bullet in the neck – a superficial wound which his mother would tend.

With the exception of this future specialist in insurrection, students were absent from these events. It is not easy, moreover, to discern who exactly the rioters were. The vocabulary of the officers and police varies over time: first of all they mention 'adolescents', almost children, then 'vagabonds', and finally 'workers'. What appears clearly, however, is the spontaneous character of the rising, without leaders or goal: a joyous demonstration that 'degenerated', as would be said today. At all events, this was the first time in a long while (since the royalist uprising of 13 Vendémiaire year III) that soldiers had opened fire on Parisians.

The following day, 20 November, reports in the newspapers led a still greater number of curious spectators into the quarter. 'At dusk, many groups of individuals seeming to belong to the working class were stationed on the boulevard at the junctions with the rues Saint-Denis and Saint-Martin, and at the corner of the main streets crossing them.' The barricades demolished the day before were raised again. 'Not a scrap of the materials they were made from had been removed: the planks, beams, cobbles and paving-stones were still in the same place.' Three barricades blocked the rue Saint-Denis by the passage du Grand-Cerf, the Saint-Leu church and the mouth of the rue Grenétat.

Deployed like the previous day at the Porte Saint-Denis and the Châtelet, the troops attacked at around eleven at night. They were faced this time with rioters who were more determined and aggressive. 'But what enemies had they been sent to fight? Unarmed citizens, celebrating the elections whose result was challenged by the army of a regime that was no less a burden to them than to the population.' Several officers, in fact, refused to obey the order to open fire, replying that they did not want to 'trade bullets for stones'. Colonel Fitz-James, however, who commanded the troops of the line, wrote in his report that, on arrival in the rue Grenétat, 'At a distance of about fifty yards we perceived a strong barricade, from behind which the crowd's shouts could be heard, and before we could clearly make out the insults and provocations, stones began to reach the advance party and gave us positive warning of those behind the barricades.' Fitz-James gave the order to fire, the barricade was overturned, the cavalry charged through the adjacent streets, and four people were killed. At two in the morning, calm was restored. Delavau, the prefect of police, concluded: 'The events of this evening inspired a healthy fear in the quarter, which we must hope will prevent the return of similar disorders.'

It was not long before this hope was disappointed. The barricades of November 1827 today appear as a rehearsal of the play that would be staged less than three years later on the barricades of July 1830. These marked the high point, and it is no accident that the most famous painting of an episode in the history of France – *Liberty Guiding the People* – was made by Delacroix after the Three Glorious Days. This painting shows what it is that permits us to speak of an *apogee*: in the heat of the action, alongside Liberty we see amid the smoke a worker, a student and a youngster, three types who fought side by side, as all witnesses concur. In these *journées*, the whole population of Paris was present on the barricades, with the exception of the aristocracy and haute bourgeoisie. And the obstacle was used to maximum tactical effect: the army units, immobilized and cut off from one another in the tight network of barricades, were unable to either advance or retreat, hemmed in by an offensive movement in a perimeter that was reduced by the hour until restricted to the Louvre and the Tuileries.

Two exceptional witnesses – or rather, two actors – have related these events. The first, sombre and melancholic, watched the crumbling of a dynasty he had always supported, despite denouncing its baseness and mistakes: Chateaubriand. The second joyously went to buy a rifle and bullets as soon as the events got under way: Alexandre Dumas.[5]

After the resignation of the Villèle ministry, and an inconsistent succession under Martignac, the king appointed the prince de Polignac to the post of prime minister in August 1829. Son of a favourite of Marie-Antoinette, a former émigré, ultra-royalist, a member of the lay Catholic organization La Congrégation, Polignac added to these reasons for his unpopularity a detestable choice of ministers. For the *Journal des débats*, a fairly moderate newspaper, this team represented: 'Coblenz, Waterloo, 1815. . . . If you twist and squeeze this ministry, only humiliation, unhappiness and danger will drop from it' (15 August 1829).

The liberal opposition gathered strength throughout France. To a threatening speech from the throne delivered by Charles X in 1830, the liberals voted a response known as the 'Address of the 221'. The Charter, they wrote, had made the agreement of the government and the people the condition for public affairs to follow a proper course. 'Sire, our loyalty, our devotion, compel us to tell you that this agreement does not exist.' They concluded by demanding the resignation of the Polignac ministry. The king and his entourage, preoccupied as they were by preparing for the Algiers expedition, did not heed this request and decided to dissolve the Chamber.

The elections held at the beginning of July 1830 gave a large majority to the opposition, which won 274 seats as against 143 for supporters for the ministry. Charles X and Polignac were not prepared to bow to the country's vote, still less when bolstered by the

---

5   Alexandre Dumas, *Mémoires* (Paris: Michel-Lévy, 1863), pp. 82–6. Unreferenced quotations are taken from these pages.

news of the taking of Algiers, which reached Paris on 9 July. They resolved to apply article 14 of the Charter, which granted the king the right to legislate by decree 'for the exercise of the law and the safety of the state' (a provision that persists almost unchanged in the present French constitution, as article 16).

In the late morning of 26 July, *Le Moniteur* published the famous decrees, five in number. As Chateaubriand wrote, 'the secret was so well kept that neither the maréchal duc de Raguse [Marmont], major-general of the guard, nor M. Mangin, the prefect of police, were taken into confidence.' The first decree suspended freedom of the press. The second dissolved the Chamber of Deputies that had just been elected. The third restricted the electoral body by halving the number of deputies and limiting the electors to a small number of proprietors, the highest taxpayers in each department. The two final decrees settled the date of future elections and announced various appointments. The glove had been thrown down, the crown had violated the Charter: it was a coup d'état.

That afternoon a large number of journalists and political figures met in the offices of *Le National*, on the rue Saint-Marc.[6] It was decided to continue the newspaper despite the ban. Thiers wrote a protest which stated in part: 'Today therefore the government has violated legality. We are dispensed from obeying; we shall try to publish our papers without asking the authorization that is imposed on us.'[7] Forty-five of those present signed the protest, which was then printed in thousands of copies and distributed in the streets.

------

6 *Le National* had been founded in January 1830, with funds from the banker Laffitte. Published by the Sautelet bookstore, it contained articles signed among others by Adolphe Thiers, Armand Carrel and François Mignet – some of these moderate republicans, others Orleanists (supporters of the future Louis-Philippe).

7 Vaulabelle, *Histoire des deux Restaurations*, p. 190.

In the evening, groups emerged from the Palais-Royal to cries of 'Long live the Charter! Down with Polignac!' Heading for the ministry of foreign affairs on the boulevard des Capucines, they arrived at the same moment as Polignac himself. Stones were hurled at his carriage, windows of the ministry building broken, but the gendarmes easily dispersed the demonstrators. 'This incident could not ruffle the calm of M. Polignac; informed by the police commissioner of the Bourse that government stocks had fallen, he replied: "That's nothing; they will rise again; and had I capital available, I would not hesitate to buy them." '[8] As for the king, he was out hunting at Rambouillet.

The following day, 27 July, saw a large number of unemployed printing workers in the streets from daybreak, as the majority of proprietors had closed their newspapers. This mass of furious men spread across the city, voicing threats against the government and the ministers. Soon, Vaulabelle wrote, 'the customary course of business was suspended; shops emptied and stalls were abandoned, likewise casting into the streets a large number of young assistants and employees who were joined around one o'clock by students of law and medicine, and the pupils of the *grandes écoles*.'[9] The print workers stood on bollards and read the protest of the journalists to passers-by. One item of news increased the anger of the crowd: that Marmont, duc de Raguse, was heading the troops massed in Paris, a despised man whose defection in 1814 was in everyone's memory (the very word *ragusade* had come to stand for treason).

Resistance firmed up in the central quarters, around the Bourse and the Palais-Royal. Mounted gendarmes cleared the gardens of the Palais, but a dense crowd remained in the side streets. Around three in the afternoon, at the entrance to the rue du Lycée [between the

---

8   Ibid., p. 198.

9   Ibid., p. 205. It is Vaulabelle who gives the most detailed description of the days of July 1830.

present rue de Valois and rue des Bons-Enfants], the troops opened fire; one man fell dead and three others were wounded, those around them fleeing with cries of 'Vengeance! To arms!' The gendarmes pressed the crowd back to the place Vendôme and charged the groups assembled in front of the hôtel belonging to one of the leaders of the parlementary opposition, Casimir Périer. Some thirty deputies were gathered inside, waiting for advice and orders. Their expectation would soon be disappointed: 'M. Casimir Périer,' wrote Chateaubriand, 'a man of order and wealth, did not wish to fall into the hands of the people; he still cherished the hope of coming to an arrangement with the legitimate monarchy; he said sharply to M. de Schonen: "You are ruining your chances by going against the law; you are forcing us out of a superb position." '[10]

During this meeting, the crowd, swollen by the news of casualties and fatalities, surged to the Palais-Royal. Vehicles loaded with bricks and stones intended for a building site tried to enter the rue de Rohan from the rue Saint-Honoré. Dumas explains:

> Étienne Arago returned to the Théâtre du Vaudeville, which was then on the rue de Chartres, when a detachment of troops blocked his path on the rue Saint-Honoré, opposite the Delorme arcade. People said that a man had just been killed on the rue du Lycée. A cart filled with rubble was waiting to pass until the troops dispersed, followed by four or five vehicles that were likewise stopped by the same obstacle.
>
> 'Excuse me, friend,' said Étienne to the driver, while he detached the shafts, 'we need your vehicle.'
> 'But why?'
> 'To make a barricade, of course!'

---

10   Casimir Périer, future prime minister under Louis-Philippe, would die in the cholera outbreak of 1832. François-René de Chateaubriand, *Memoirs from Beyond the Tomb* (London: Penguin, 2014), p. 359.

'Yes, yes, barricades! Barricades!' several voices echoed.

In a brief moment, the horses were unhitched, the cart turned on its side, and the rubble arranged across the street.[11]

A few yards away, in the rue de l'Échelle, a group of people seized a bus and a water-carrier's vehicle, to make a second barricade. Mounted gendarmes were driven back by stones, but they finally managed to circumvent the barricades and disperse the crowd without a shot being fired.

To maintain order in Paris Marmont disposed of some 15,000 men, Swiss and French guards as well as troops of the line. In the afternoon he sent them to a number of positions between the place Louis-XVI [now de la Concorde] and the Bastille, with strong points at the Palais-Royal, place Vendôme, on the boulevards and the Pont Neuf. These detachments were ordered to communicate with one another by messenger, to patrol the streets and clear away everything they might find as they went. In the outlying quarters the troops met with little resistance, but around the Palais-Royal the crowd flooded the streets, new barricades were built, and stones flew from all sides. As the soldiers advanced, the crowd closed ranks behind them. The detachment was forced to fire in order to free itself, killing four men on the rue Traversière.[12]

The end of the evening saw the appearance of the first firearms – pistols and hunting rifles. Dumas returned home at night:

In the rue de l'Échelle, shadows of some kind moved in the dark. I approached; at the cry of 'Who goes there?' I replied 'A friend!', and continued to advance. It was a barricade being silently raised, as if it had been built by the spirits of the night. I shook hands with these night-time workers and proceeded to the Carrousel.

---

11   Étienne Arago was the brother of François Arago, the famous astronomer. That evening he went from theatre to theatre to have them closed.

12   This met the rue Saint-Honoré opposite the rue de l'Échelle.

From five in the morning of the next day, 28 July, groups began to assemble at all the city crossroads. Many men were armed with hunting rifles, swords, sabres or pistols. Others, armed with building tools, removed paving-stones from the streets to build barricades. More barricades were seen in these days than ever before: 4,000 according to Chateaubriand, a figure confirmed by Traugott who notes that such a density corresponded to one barricade for every 200 Parisians – men, women and children.[13]

The court suppliers generally displayed the royal arms on their shop signs. As Chateaubriand wrote: 'The mob pulled down and burnt the French arms; they hung them from the ropes of the shattered street-lamps; they tore the fleur-de-lis badges from the uniforms of the diligence guards and the postmen; the notaries removed their escutcheons, the bailiffs their badges, the carriers their official signs, the Court purveyors their warrants.'[14] After a few hours, all reminders of the reign of the Bourbons had disappeared. The dominant cry was no longer 'Long live the Charter!' but rather '*Vive la liberté! Down with the ministers! Down with the Bourbons!*'

Marmont, still at Saint-Cloud, sent the king a letter expressing his disquiet: 'It is no longer a riot, it is a revolution. It is urgent that Your Majesty take measures of pacification. The honour of the crown can still be saved; tomorrow perhaps it will be too late.' But instead he received from the king and Polignac a formal order of repression. Paris was placed under a state of siege, concentrating all military power under Marmont. 'M. le duc de Raguse,' wrote Chateaubriand, 'a man of intelligence and merit, a brave soldier and a clever but unlucky general, proved for the thousandth time that military genius is not enough to deal with civil disturbances: any police officer would have known better than the marshal what had to be done. Perhaps

---

13   Mark Traugott, *The Insurgent Barricade* (Berkeley, CA: University of California Press, 2010), p. 105.

14   Chateaubriand, *Memoirs from Beyond the Tomb*, p. 361.

too his mind was paralysed by his memories; he remained as it were stifled by the weight of the fatality of his name.'[15]

Marmont launched four columns from his headquarters at the Carrousel. The first received the order to occupy the place de l'Hôtel-de-Ville, proceeding via the quays. The second was to clear the rue Saint-Honoré and take up position at the Innocents market; the third was to follow the rue de Richelieu and the boulevards up to the Bastille, the fourth to proceed along the boulevards from the Madeleine to the rue de Richelieu. But everywhere barricades had been erected, defended by firing from every street corner, every window and rooftop. The insurgents crossed from the Left Bank and attacked the troops who had arrived at the Hôtel de Ville. Dumas took part in the action:

> Our two drums beat the charge and we advanced at a quick pace. We could see about a hundred men in the distance (who composed almost the entire insurgent army) marching boldly towards the bridge [the suspension bridge now replaced by the Pont Louis-Philippe], the tricolour at their head, when suddenly a piece of cannon raked the whole length of the bridge. The cannon was loaded with grapeshot and the effect was terrible. The tricolour disappeared, some eight or ten men fell, and a dozen to fifteen took flight. But the fugitives rallied again at the cries of those who remained unmoved on the bridge. From our sheltered position by the parapet we fired on the gunners. Two of them fell.

The troops could do no better than hold the ground where they were pinned down, both at the Innocents market and the place de la Bastille. A detachment of cavalry from the latter position tried to reach the Hôtel de Ville via the rue Saint-Antoine, defended by several barricades. But 'tiles, paving-stones, logs, furniture, broken

---

15 Ibid., p. 362.

bottles, hurled from every window and roof, wounded or killed the men, frightening or laming their horses, and this soon brought the cavalry to a halt and forced them to withdraw, leaving a large number of dead or wounded on the ground.'

From the Bastille, the troops tried to escape through the boulevards, but large trees had been cut down and 'formed several hundred armed barricades right along the boulevards between the faubourg Saint-Antoine and the Italiens quarter, in all directions, with long and thick branches that made them impossible to cross, even for the infantry.'[16]

By two in the afternoon, the troops were encircled at the Hôtel de Ville, the Innocents market, the Porte Saint-Denis and the Bastille. They were short of supplies and munitions. Marmont sent the king a message: 'The troops could not run the risk of being trapped in their positions, but I must not conceal from you that the situation is serious.' François Arago, followed by a group of deputies who included Casimir Périer and Jacques Laffitte, sought out the marshal to convince him to order a ceasefire. Emissaries were sent to Saint-Cloud to try to stop the bloodshed, but the king replied: 'I have the same trust in my arms and in my right. I will not and must not deal with subjects in rebellion. Let them lay down their arms; they are familiar enough with my goodness to be sure of the most generous pardon.'

During these discussions the position of the troops became increasingly untenable. In places, officers refused to open fire, and there were growing signs of fraternization between the soldiers of the line – despised by the guards and less well treated – and the insurgents. This is one of the effects of a war of barricades: the moment of tension before confrontation is propitious for discussions in which the insurgents may be able to convince the soldiers to put an end to a fratricidal struggle.

---

16   Vaulabelle, *Histoire des deux Restaurations*, pp. 240–1.

At nightfall, Marmont received the order to regroup his harassed forces around the Louvre and the Tuileries. The retreat was difficult on account of an unwillingness to abandon the wounded, and the difficulty that the artillery had in crossing the barricades. In the words of Chateaubriand, 'When the troops returned from the different quarters of Paris, they believed that the king and the dauphin had likewise arrived from their side: looking in vain for the white flag on the Pavillon de l'Horloge [Tuileries], they erupted in barrack-room language.'

At dawn on 29 July, Marmont's troops were concentrated in a long quadrilateral bordered on one side by the Seine and on the other by the axis of the rue Saint-Honoré, with the Louvre to the east and the place Louis-XVI to the west. 'This position is unchallengeable,' Marmont had said the previous day. 'I shall hold it for three weeks.'[17] The people were now masters of the city; they had spent the night building barricades, 'every twenty paces' according to Chateaubriand, around the entrenched camp that was closed on three sides and open only towards the Champs-Élysées.

After inspecting his advance positions, Marmont decided to summon the Paris mayors in order to press the king to a compromise. While waiting, he wrote a short proclamation to the people of Paris in which he proposed, 'out of humanity, to suspend hostilities', but there was no way to have it printed. Handwritten copies were distributed here and there, to no effect. Outside, however, the attack was being prepared.

On the Left Bank, which had up to now been outside the fighting, groups formed at the Odéon, receiving the support of École polytechnique students mobilized by Charras – an erstwhile classmate who had been expelled for singing the *Marseillaise*.[18] These

---

17   Ibid., p. 273.

18   The *polytechniciens* were popular in Paris. Their heroic conduct on 30 March 1814 was remembered when they defended the Trône barrier against the

insurgents, who included a number of former *carbonari*, tried to attack the Louvre from the Pont Royal, but they were repelled by artillery fire. Two battalions of Swiss guards were defending the palace; one of them, stationed under the colonnade, aimed a downward fire at the assailants, who fired back from the church of Saint-Germain-l'Auxerrois and the adjacent houses; the other, posted beneath the gateway opposite the Institut de France, fired on the Left Bank insurgents who were trying to reach the Pont des Arts.

Meanwhile Marmont was still doing his utmost to put an end to the fighting. Four mayors had responded to his appeal. He sent them to his outposts to announce a truce, when suddenly a tremendous clamour was heard: it was learned that the 5th and 53rd regiments of the line, positioned on the place Vendôme, had gone over to the rebel side. A gaping hole opened in Marmont's disposition of forces. He hastily sent one of the two Swiss battalions along the rue de Rivoli to the Louvre, to block the rue de Castiglione. The officer in command of those Swiss who had remained at the Louvre made a clumsy manoeuvre that left the Louvre momentarily unprotected. Then:

> A boy emboldened by the momentary ceasing of rifle fire and the disappearance of the defenders of the colonnade approached a buttress that came down very steeply from this colonnade to the ground, climbed onto it and reached the galleries that the Swiss had just abandoned. He entered the apartments and showed himself to the soldiers; at which sight a cry arose in the midst of this dismayed band: 'The people are in the Louvre!' The battalion was seized by a frightful terror; officers and soldiers alike fled in disorder towards the gateway leading to the Carrousel, and hastened pell-mell to the Tuileries.[19]

Allies (see Eric Hazan, 'Le 30 mars 1814', *Paris sous tension*, Paris: La Fabrique, 2010).

19   Vaulabelle, *Histoire des deux Restaurations*, pp. 286–7.

The unfortunate Swiss clearly still remembered the massacre of their compatriots in the same place on 10 August 1792.

Upon seeing the rout of the Swiss guards, the insurgents massed on the Left Bank surged across the Pont Royal towards the Tuileries, climbing to the top of the Pavillon de Flore, where they raised the tricolour flag. Marmont had no choice but to reunite what was left of his troops and retreat along the Champs-Élysées towards the Bois de Boulogne. Charles X would soon depart for exile in England.

To cite Alexandre Dumas again:

> Thus the Revolution of 1830 was accomplished, not by those cautious actors of the past fifteen years' comedy who hid in the wings while the people played that bloody three days' drama; not by Casimir Périer, Laffitte, Benjamin Constant, Sebastiani, Guizot, Mauguin, Choiseul, Odilon Berrot and the three Dupins. These actors were not even in the wings. That would have been too near the stage. They were hermetically sealed at home. The only mention of resistance from them was one legally organized. While the Louvre and Tuileries were being taken, they were in their drawing-rooms, discussing terms which many of them even then considered too bold.

But it was the 'cautious actors' who would draw the chestnuts out of the fire. The Orleanists attracted the moderate republicans to their party, and together, making use of the aged Lafayette, they stole the victory that the people had won on the barricades, placing the duc d'Orléans on the throne under the name of Louis-Philippe I. But the frustrated people would not be long in reacting, and in the years that followed, they would resume the battle on new barricades.

Chapter 5

The First Proletarian Barricades: Lyon, November 1831 and April 1834

'We have shaken off the yoke of the noble aristocracy only to fall under the domination of the financial aristocracy, we have expelled our parchment tyrants only to fling ourselves into the arms of the millionaire despots. Our lot, accordingly, could not improve; the old ones despised us because we could not cite illustrious ancestors, and the new ones disdain us because we have not been favoured by fortune.' That is how Auguste Colin, a typographer, expressed himself in 1831, in his newspaper *Le Cri du peuple*.[1]

It was in Lyon that the anger of the poor found expression for the first time after the revolution of 1830. This was no accident: Lyon was the largest industrial town in France, with half of its 180,000 inhabitants making their living from silk-weaving. 'La Fabrique', as it was known, 'the manufactory', was the property of 'manufacturers', who made nothing at all but were entrepreneurs or capitalists. They supplied the raw material, that is, silk, to the workshop masters whom they paid by the piece. The master was the owner of the looms. He himself wove on one of these, entrusting the others to journeymen who received an average wage of half the price of the finished item. The majority of the

---

1   Cited in *La Parole ouvrière*, texts collected and edited by Alain Faure and Jacques Rancière (Paris: La Fabrique, 2007).

masters, who had only three or four looms, were semi-proletarians, who rapidly united with their journeymen in the conflicts.

In 1830 the silk workers, known as *canuts*, still lived in the old Saint-Georges quarter, but increasing numbers of them had moved to the heights of La Croix-Rousse, in housing barracks that had been built specially for them. These weavers worked fifteen or eighteen hours a day for a wretched wage. The prefect wrote to the minister of commerce: 'There is real suffering among the 60,000 to 80,000 workers. Unless a cruel decision is made to kill them all, we cannot respond to the peaceful expression of their needs by rifle fire.'[2]

This expression would become less peaceful around the question of the *tarif*: journeymen and masters tried to impose on the 'manufacturers' a minimum price per piece. The prefect managed to get them to accept the principle, but the 'manufacturers', pleading poverty, soon attempted to renege: 'The great mistake made by the prefect has placed the industrialists in a terrible position,' they said.[3] Their response to strike movements was a lockout, and within a few days thousands of looms ceased to operate for lack of silk and orders.

On Sunday, 20 November 1831, the workshop masters and journeymen, assembled on the place de la Croix-Rousse, decided on a peaceful demonstration throughout the city the next day to demand the *tarif* – and work. On the morning of the 21st, numerous groups formed on the hilltop. A detachment of National Guard, made up of 'manufacturers' and clerks, was welcomed with a hail of stones and had to beat a hasty retreat. The National Guard of La Croix-Rousse (which was at the time a separate commune) had their rifles with them, and the workers also began to arm. The prefect and the general in command of the Lyon National Guard proceeded to La Grand-Côte and tried to parlay, but the overexcited workers surrounded

---

2   Cited in Jacques Perdu, *La Révolte des canuts, 1831–1834* [1931] (Paris: Spartacus, 1974), p. 17.

3   Ibid., p. 27.

them, scattered their escort with rifle fire, took them prisoner and brought them to the *mairie* of La Croix-Rousse.

In the course of the day, the army tried to gain a foothold in the plain east of the city, but their cavalry charges came up against barricades constructed in these narrow, crooked and winding streets, from which a rain of stones and tiles fell upon the horses. The soldiers fought only half-heartedly, particularly those of the line, who in some places refused to fire on the workers. In the evening the prefect was released, and the general exchanged for workers who had been taken prisoner. Workers from Les Brotteaux and La Guillotière, who had taken a long detour by the north from the left bank of the Rhône, came to reinforce their comrades of La Croix-Rousse. At nightfall the advantage was on the side of the insurgents.

The next morning, a great crowd assembled to descend into the city, carrying a black flag bearing the famous motto: 'Live working or die fighting'. The authorities tried to mobilize the National Guard, but the majority of these citizen soldiers refused to enforce order. The drums beating the alarm were attacked, officers were injured or threatened. The insurrection spread to the whole city. In the faubourgs, La Guillotière, Saint-Just, Les Brotteaux, all trades downed tools and the workers joined the insurgents. While the army tried to make its way up to La Croix-Rousse, the streets, squares and quays were covered with barricades. The workers gradually focused on the National Guards of the party of order and the troops in the city centre. From La Guillotière, they crossed the Rhône and occupied the place Bellecour. Those from Les Brotteaux crossed the Pont Morand and reached the vicinity of the Hôtel de Ville, which was encircled on all sides.

At midnight, Roguet, the general in command of the army, decided to abandon the city. The retreat across the barricades was bloody, and the troops had to leave their dead and wounded behind. At three in the morning, the workers entered the Hôtel de Ville. Lyon was in the hands of the insurgents.

Next day a 'provisional general staff' was formed at the Hôtel de Ville, grouping the leaders of the insurgent workers with militant republicans. The aim was to replace the traditional authorities with leaders appointed by the workers: 'Lyon, gloriously liberated by its sons, must have magistrates of its own choice, magistrates whose robes are not soiled with the blood of their brothers!'[4] But in the days

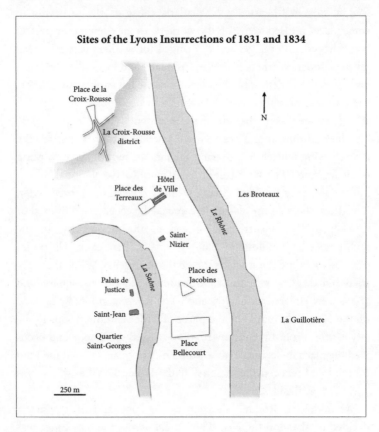

Sites of the Lyons Insurrections of 1831 and 1834

Place de la Croix-Rousse

La Croix-Rousse district

N

Place des Terreaux

Hôtel de Ville

Les Broteaux

Le Rhône

Saint-Nizier

Place des Jacobins

Palais de Justice

La Saône

Saint-Jean

La Guillotière

Quartier Saint-Georges

Place Bellecourt

250 m

4 Proclamation cited in Fernand Rude, *Les Révoltes des canuts (1831–1834)* (Paris: La Découverte, 2007), p. 47.

that followed, dissensions and the lack of a political vision would prevent the consolidation of victory. The government concentrated a veritable army at the city gates, headed by the prince d'Orléans, heir to the throne, and maréchal Soult, the minister of war. The Lyon National Guard was dissolved. The workers let themselves be disarmed, and gradually went back to work. On 3 December the army made its entry into the faubourg of Vaise, the workers' leaders were arrested, and order reigned in the city.

But not for long. In the following months Lyon was racked by an agitation which now became openly political. The workers founded the Société des Ferrandiniers, a secret association that became a centre of republican propaganda. The cooperative movement and the Saint-Simonians launched a newspaper by share subscription, *L'Écho de la Fabrique*, which became the organ of the city's working class. In September 1833 a Lyon section of the Société des Droits de l'Homme was founded, uniting the most combative republican elements: not only workers, but also intellectuals and students, including many followers of Babeuf, who were in touch with their Paris comrades.[5]

In February 1834, the manufacturers announced a reduction of 25 centimes per *aune* [approx. 1.37 metres] of plush. The workers immediately reacted – not just those directly affected by this measure, but the whole Fabrique. On 12 February, a meeting of more than 2,000 masters voted for a strike, and some 20,000 looms immediately came to a halt. Other corporations, particularly the typographers, opened a subscription in support of the strikers, but the manufacturers and the prefect held firm, and work resumed at the end of the month.

In the wake of this strike, six leaders were arrested. Their trial was set for 5 April. On that day, the workers descended en masse from La Croix-Rousse and the Saint-Georges quarter to the Palais de Justice, occupying the surroundings and the court itself. The president of the

---

5   The Babouvists included Filippo Buonarroti, Charles Teste and Voyet d'Argenson, who spread the ideas of Robespierre and Gracchus Babeuf.

tribunal sent for reinforcements, but when the soldiers appeared the crowd cheered them, and soon troopers and workers were drinking together in the courtyard. The magistrates and court gendarmes escaped through a window.[6]

On 9 April, the day to which the trial had been postponed, the city was under military occupation: artillery, cavalry and troops of the line were placed at strategic positions, the bridges were blocked, dragoons patrolled the streets. Proclamations were distributed, read out by workers who climbed on bollards, urging the dismissal of Louis-Philippe and calling for insurrection. At the end of the morning, barricades were constructed, first of all around the place Saint-Jean and the court building, then throughout the city. The workers hoped to fraternize with the troops, but the soldiers furiously attacked the hastily constructed barricades, defended by poorly armed men. La Croix-Rousse was transformed into an entrenched camp by a whole network of barricades, but the workers did not manage to descend into the city. Fighting continued throughout the day in the city centre, at Saint-Nizier and Les Cordeliers. In the workers' quarter of old Lyon, on the right bank of the Saône, all the streets were barricaded. The troops fired on inhabitants who came out of their homes, or at windows if a face appeared. The insurgents were isolated, as the troops had occupied the Rhône bridges, preventing workers from Les Brotteaux and La Guillotière from coming to their aid as in 1831. Despite this they held firm in the face of a hellish fire, and spent the night behind the barricades.

Over the following days the insurgents, conscious of their inferiority in numbers and weapons, waged a guerrilla campaign: they sniped from windows and roofs, withdrawing when troops appeared. As soon as one barricade was taken, another replaced it. But the vice steadily tightened. On 12 April, the fourth day of the insurrection, the

---

6   This and the following day are described in detail in Perdu, *La Révolte des canuts*, pp. 65–84.

troops launched a convergent assault on the centre, where the republicans still held out around the Saint-Nizier and Saint-Bonaventure churches. Insurgents were killed even inside the churches. A priest who witnessed the massacre wrote: 'Bodies bloody and disfigured by gunfire, the metal of bayonets, broken trunks, altars and tabernacles destroyed, soldiers red with rage (some with drink), fires still burning, a thick smoke throughout the church, a confused and terrible noise of voices, shouts, cries, blasphemies, and blood, blood everywhere!'[7] On 15 April, the last shots rang out in La Croix-Rousse.

Throughout these days, troops fired on civilians and slaughtered at random, including women and children. The press of the 'happy medium' celebrated the victory and sang the praises of the army. The prefect, Gasparin, was made a peer of France, and the general in command of the troops, Aymar, received the *grand cordon* of the Légion d'honneur. A special court was formed to judge the hundreds of arrested insurgents. But it was not to be forgotten how in the course of this first proletarian insurrection a small number of poorly armed workers, without a central command, managed with their barricades to keep 8,000 men at bay for a week. 'This handful of brave men', wrote one of the *canuts*, 'could not have held out for more than twenty-four hours for the sake of any cause other than that of the republic.'[8]

---

7   Ibid., p. 157.

8   Cited in Rude, *Les Révoltes des canuts*, p. 166.

Chapter 6

Barricades in the Age of Romanticism: June 1832

Chateaubriand and Balzac, Dumas and George Sand, Heine and Victor Hugo: all of these, at one time or another, wrote about the barricades of June 1832, that heroic and desperate battle waged by those who refused to accept the theft of the revolution of 1830.

The republicans were organized: the Société des Amis du Peuple, the Société des Droits de l'Homme, the Société Gauloise and the Réclamants de Juillet grouped the most active of those who were not content with the speeches and protests of the legal opposition. Bonapartists and Legitimists also agitated and took part in the insurrectionary *journées*.

The anger of the people had been rising since a terrible cholera epidemic in March had killed, at its worst, over a thousand people a day. Many celebrities died, including Cuvier, Champollion and the prime minister himself, Casimir Périer. Eminent physicians such as Magendie, Récamier, Dupuytren, Larrey and Broussais prescribed remedies ranging from ice baths to leeches, opium, blood-letting and various fumigations. But the glaring fact was that the disease struck hardest at the poor: the mortality rate was between eight and nine people per thousand in the elegant quarters, rising to over fifty per thousand 'in the quarters of the Hôtel de Ville and the Cité, the abodes of penury'.[1] Poisoners were rumoured to be spreading death everywhere. The majority of the rich fled the city; the deputies fled, the peers of France fled 'with a train of doctors and pharmacies', according to Heine, Paris correspondent of the *Augsburger Zeitung*. 'The poor note with discontent that money has become a protection against death.'[2]

Tension came to a head when the newspapers announced the death of General Lamarque. A nineteen-year-old volunteer at the time of the Revolution, he had fought at Hohenlinden and Wagram as well as in Spain. Banished after the Hundred Days, a patriot and a liberal, in favour of war for the emancipation of peoples, Lamarque was a popular deputy. His family announced that the funeral would take place on 5 June: mourners were to meet at their house on the rue Saint-Honoré, from which the coffin would be taken to the Barrière d'Italie before proceeding to Mont-de-Marsan, the hero's native town. Republicans took this as the opportunity for an action.

On 5 June it was raining, but from eight in the morning there was a dense crowd around Lamarque's home. National Guards in uniform were to be seen (artillery in particular, traditionally republican), workers, students and old soldiers. On the place de la Concorde, students from the law and medicine faculties mingled with members of the Société des Amis du Peuple, forming into squadrons and selecting their leaders. The government, for its part, took precautions: carabineers were positioned around the place de la Concorde and troops of the line on the place de l'Hôtel-de-Ville, the place de la Bastille and in the Latin Quarter, while the 6th regiment of dragoons was at the Célestins barracks near the Arsenal – a total of more than 20,000 men.

---

1   Louis Blanc, *History of Ten Years 1830–1840* (London: Chapman & Hall, 1844), vol. 1, p. 618. This gives a detailed account of the June days of 1832.

2   'French Affairs', *Works of Heinrich Heine*, vol. 8 (London: Heinemann, 1893), p. 176.

At eleven o'clock, the door decked with black was opened for the passage of the coffin. This was escorted by Lafayette, Laffitte, the Bonapartist General Clausel and Mauguin, an opposition advocate. The procession advanced via the Madeleine and the boulevards, but on reaching the rue de la Paix, a shout was heard: 'Around the column with the soldier of Napoleon!' A right turn, therefore, and the coffin made three rounds of the place Vendôme, where soldiers at the offices of the general staff were obliged to render military honours. The procession then continued along the boulevards:

> That immense population, crowding every balcony, filling every window, weighing down every tree, covering every house-top, those flags, Italian, Polish, German, Spanish, recalling to the minds of all who saw them so many tyrannies triumphant, so many insults unavenged; those too manifest preparations for battle; those very precautions of a government whose conscience taught it to see danger even in the passage of a dead man to his last home; the revolutionary hymns rising into the air amidst menacing cries and the mournful roll of the muffled drum, all this disposed the minds of men to an excitement full of peril.[3]

Just as the coffin reached the place de la Bastille, some sixty students from the Polytechnique came running. They had ignored the order not to leave the school and were ready to join the insurrection. (We may remember the opening words of Stendhal's second novel: 'Lucien Leuwen had been expelled from the Polytechnique for having gone for an inappropriate walk, one day when he and all his fellow students were detained: this was the time of one of the famous *journées* of June, April or February 1832 or 1834.') The procession followed the boulevard Bourdon, between the Arsenal basin and the

---

3 Blanc, *History of Ten Years*, vol. 2, p. 30.

grain warehouses, crossed the little bridge at the end of the canal and stopped on the esplanade just before the Pont d'Austerlitz.

A podium had been erected here for valdedictory speeches by Lafayette, Marshal Clausel, and foreign generals. The tail end of the great crowd was still at the Bastille; there was growing restlessness. Suddenly a strange horseman appeared, dressed in black; he passed slowly along the ranks, holding a red flag topped by a Phrygian cap, on which the words could be read: 'Liberty or death'. This image of 1793 electrified the crowd, but terrified those officiating on the podium: Lafayette hastened off in a fiacre, and General Exelmans, who attempted to object, narrowly escaped being thrown into the canal.

At this point a small detachment of dragoons from the Célestins barracks arrived on the quai Morland.[4] The crowd booed them and pelted them with stones, a shot was fired, and the battle began. This time a whole squadron emerged from the barracks, surging through the rue de la Cerisaie and charging the crowd. From the granaries and the Arsenal, the insurgents fired on the dragoons. The colonel's horse was killed under him. A barricade, the first of the day, was hastily erected on the boulevard Bourdon, and the dragoons had to withdraw into their barracks.

Meanwhile some young people had crossed the Pont d'Austerlitz with the coffin, and reached the Jardin des Plantes. Here a carriage was waiting to take the general to his last resting-place in the Landes, but the insurgents shouted out: 'To the Panthéon!' The carabineers who tried to block their path were met by rifle fire. The rioters took possession of the veterans' barracks, stormed the guard post on the

---

4   There is still a cavalry barracks on the boulevard Henri-IV. At that time the Célestins barracks was on the rue du Petit-Musc; the present barracks dates from the late nineteenth century. Regarding the quai Morland, the Louviers island was not yet connected to the Right Bank, and the Arsenal library was on the embankment, fronted by this quay.

place Maubert, and occupied the entire line of the barriers on the Left Bank.[5] On the opposite bank, their advance was equally rapid: the guard posts of the Marais, the *mairie* of the eighth arrondissement, the post of the Château-d'Eau and the Les Halles quarter were in their hands.[6]

Paris was already enflamed. The republicans had spread themselves in every direction, running up barricades in the different streets, disarming the military posts, summoning the troops whom they came across to join them, attacking them if they refused, menacing the powder magazines and arsenals, arresting the drummers whom they found beating the roll-call, knocking in the drumheads; a party everywhere small in number, but constantly gaining adherents by their audacious bravery, and everywhere acting in concert. There was never anything comparable with the rapidity of this whole affair: in three hours after the first attack, one half of Paris was in the power of the insurgents.[7]

By eight in the evening, a barricade had been erected near the little bridge of the Hôtel-Dieu, and the troops retreated along the quai aux Fleurs. The prefecture of police was completely encircled.[8]

The government was reluctant to get engaged in a battle of streets and alleys, as had been fatal to Marmont's troops in 1830. Soult, the

---

5   The veterans' barracks was on the rue Mouffetard, close to the rue de l'Épée-de-Bois.

6   The eighth arrondissement included the faubourg Saint-Antoine and the east of the Marais. The town hall was on the place Royale [now des Vosges]. The Château-d'Eau was close to the present place de la République.

7   Blanc, *History of Ten Years*, vol. 2, p. 33.

8   The Hôtel-Dieu was built on the Île de la Cité, facing the Seine, with an extension on the Left Bank to which it was connected by a bridge. The prefecture of police was at the point of the Île de la Cité, in the rue de Jérusalem.

minister of war, advised a withdrawal to the Champ-de-Mars, but this was opposed by the prefect of police, Gisquet, and the decision was taken to stand and resist. Fresh troops were brought in from the Paris suburbs, as well as artillery.

The insurrectionaries established their headquarters close to the Saint-Merry church, in the Saint-Avoye quarter (now Beaubourg). A complex of barricades was constructed on the rue Saint-Martin, by house no. 30. In a letter to his sister, Charles Jeanne, who headed the resistance here, relates:

> In a moment, and as if by some enchantment, three strong barricades were raised, the first at the corner of the rue Saint-Merry continued outward and cut the rue Saint-Martin at a right angle; the second, also at a right angle to the former, blocked the rue Aubry-le-Boucher; and finally the third, raised at the corner of the rue Maubuée, brought this latter street within our retrenchments. A house under construction in the rue Aubry-le-Boucher facilitated the execution of our means of defence; wooden scaffolding and rubble, along with paving-stones that were constantly being taken up, were piled up at prodigious speed; a large quantity of rubble, carried on people's backs in scuttles that were found in the building, was used to fill the gaps and consolidate the work. A very large flour cart that we had overturned and filled with cobbles made up around half of the Saint-Merry barricade. Finally, two hours later, our first two barricades were nearly six feet thick and five feet high, and crenelated all along their length.[9]

While the people were digging up the paving-stones, the great men of the republican opposition, would-be leaders such as Lafayette,

---

9   This letter, written by Jeanne in prison, was discovered by Thomas Bouchet, who published it in *À cinq heures nous serons tous morts* (Paris: Vendémiaire, 2011). The subsequent quotations are also taken from this work.

Laffitte, Odilon Barrot and François Arago, were divided among themselves and hesitant to play this bloody game. No name emerged to take the lead in a revolution.

During the night the battle continued to rage, but the insurgents, who were considerably outnumbered, were steadily driven from their positions. The entrenched camp of Saint-Merry, however, held fast. 'From all sides,' Jeanne wrote, 'people brought us packets of powder and some bullets; we had removed the lead from the gutters; but with all that, we had to make bullets and cartridges.' He put the young people to work and established a dressing station in the house at no. 30:

> This first duty accomplished, I kept inside the barricades forty men armed with rifles, as well as the four or five youngsters who would not abandon this post, and I divided up the rest of my brothers in

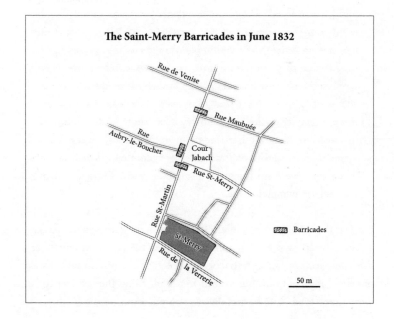

arms, almost all armed with hunting rifles and carbines, in various houses from which they could destroy a large number of our enemies by a crossfire from above, while the barricade fighters stopped them by a sustained and well-supplied fire.

At six in the evening, a column of National Guard arrived from the quays and charged into the rue Saint-Martin: 'When I stood up [Jeanne had just been wounded], the National Guard were fleeing so hastily, leaving behind their wounded, that I had only time to see to one of them who had fallen dead outright.' This first attack was scarcely repelled when another column appeared, this time from the top of the rue Saint-Martin:

> I placed all my comrades behind the Maubuée barricade, with one knee on the ground, only a few remaining at the crenelation, which was still very low [this barrier was no more than four feet high], so as to encourage the assailants by the seemingly small number of the defenders of our entrenchment. We thus let them advance until they were within pistol range, without replying to the fire that they constantly directed as they marched; but when we all suddenly rose up and gave them such a heated reception, to shouts of '*Vive la république!*', they were indecisive and stopped: this uncertainty on their part, however, was immediately followed by fresh fire from the barricade and the windows, no less well-aimed than the earlier one, which once again thinned their ranks. Then they were no longer a disciplined body, but a cloud of Cossacks in complete rout.

During this time, a very violent battle was in progress in the passage au Saumon [now rue Bachaumont, between the rue Montmartre and the rue Montorgueil]. A barricade erected at the entrance to the passage long held out, but at four in the morning the last insurgents were massacred. The barricade on the Petit-Pont of the Hôtel-Dieu was also taken, its defenders killed and thrown into the Seine. George Sand, who was living on the quay, heard 'furious clamour, tremendous cries', then there was silence. By early morning, the insurrection still held out at only two points: the entrance to the faubourg Saint-Antoine and in the Saint-Avoye quarter.

Over the day of 6 June, resistance was concentrated in the Saint-Merry pocket. Columns of National Guard attacked the barricades from all sides – from both ends of the rue Saint-Martin, from the rue Aubry-le-Boucher, from the rue de la Verrerie . . . They were all repulsed, leaving their dead and wounded behind. Around three in the afternoon, however, two cannon were positioned at the level of Saint-Nicolas-des-Champs, enfilading the rue Saint-Martin. Initially, 'the gunners fired with bullets and cast-shot; these projectiles wrought terrible damage to the shop fronts and façades of houses, but they did no great harm to our barricades.' Until the cannon advanced to the level of the rue Michel-le-Comte: 'Soon we saw our unhappy barricade [the first one, that of the rue Maubuée] shattered to pieces . . . and we were unable to defend it. . . . We took refuge in the carriage gateways adjacent to our destroyed fortifications on both sides of the street.'

The situation became critical, especially as munitions were beginning to run out. Jeanne proposed to his comrades to flee while there was still time, but all of them wanted to die at their post:

> The rue Saint-Merry was already occupied by the troops of the line; a large number of troops were advancing through the rue Saint-Martin from the quays, and to top the difficulty of an already desperate position, a cannon positioned at the end of the rue Aubry-le-Boucher was starting to fire very heavily on the crossroads by no. 30. 'My friends,' I said to those around me, 'if we go into the house we will be taken and shot; we still hold the rue Maubuée and only have facing us a company of conscripts. Let's run against them and try to break through by bayonet!'

At the head of a dozen men, Jeanne managed to break through the lines. A hail of crockery, flowerpots and household objects slowed down the pursuing soldiers ('I heard it said', wrote Jeanne, 'that even a piano had been dropped'), and the group succeeded in taking refuge in a friendly house, from where they heard the fusillade continuing. The last defenders of no. 30, those who had not been able to escape over the roofs, were massacred on the spot – like Enjolras and Grantaire in *Les Misérables*, after the barricade in the rue de la Chanverie was taken.

'It was the best blood of France that ran in the rue Saint-Martin, and I do not believe that there was better fighting at Thermopylae than at the mouth of the alley of Saint-Merry and Aubry-le-Boucher, where at the last a handful of some sixty Republicans fought against sixty thousand troops of the line and National Guards,' wrote Heine in his report of 16 June.[10]

In what has now become a tourist district, nothing, no monument or plaque, recalls the memory of these heroes of the barricades of June 1832. And yet thanks to Heine, to Hugo, even to the letter of Charles Jeanne, this remains a living memory for us.

---

10   Heine, 'French Affairs', p. 280.

Chapter 7

The Last Victorious Barricades: Paris, February 1848

It is said that on the evening of his abdication Louis-Philippe walked up and down in a trance, repeating: 'Like Charles X! Like Charles X!' He was not mistaken: the revolution of February 1848 was a reprise – though far less bloody – of the revolution of July 1830. A single spark against a background of growing discontent: the ban on a great banquet arranged by the opposition, which, for Tocqueville, 'invited the entire population to form an immense political demonstration . . . One might have taken it for a decree of the Provisional Government, which was formed three days later.'[1] The demonstration went ahead, and on the morning of 22 February a great procession got under way from the Madeleine towards Chaillot, the place chosen for the banquet, with students, workers and even opposition deputies mingling together. The column reached the place de la Concorde, singing the *Marseillaise* and shouting: 'Down with Guizot!'[2] Some young people entered the court-yard of the Palais-Bourbon, but they were swiftly expelled by dragoons and gendarmes. It was steadily raining, and the *journée* was over.

---

1   Alexis de Tocqueville, *Recollections* (London: Macdonald, 1970), p. 47. Tocqueville was elected a deputy in 1848. His account of the events of February and June is one of matchless lucidity.

2   François Guizot had headed the government since 1840.

The morning of the 23rd saw the erection of the first barricades, first of all in the old insurrectionary area between the rue Saint-Martin and the rue du Temple, then throughout the central part of the city. Workers looted armouries and helped themselves to the rifles of the National Guard. The majority of the National Guard legions refused to attack the barricades, and joined in with the shouts of 'Long live reform, down with Guizot!' Informed of these events, Louis-Philippe, who had up to then been very confident, suddenly lost his sang-froid: he dismissed Guizot and replaced him with Molé.[3] This news spread rapidly through the city, greeted with joy by the liberal bourgeoisie but less welcomed by the republicans. At ten in the evening,

> a long column of workers advanced down the boulevards by torch-light, a red flag at its head. On arriving outside the ministry of foreign affairs,[4] the unarmed crowd . . . found two companies of the line drawn up against them; then, without summons or warning, rifles were lowered and a steady fire was directed against this compact and unarmed mass.[5]

What followed is an image from revolutionary legend: the cart pulled by a white horse, the heap of bodies lit up by a torch held by a child, the circuit round the centre of Paris to shouts of 'Revenge! They're butchering the people!' The tocsin was sounded throughout the city and the insurrection became general.

---

3   Comte Molé had already been prime minister from 1836 to 1839. There was hardly any difference politically between him and Guizot, but a great personal animosity.

4   This ministry was situated on the boulevard des Capucines, at the corner with the street of that name.

5   Louis Ménard, *Prologue d'une révolution* [1848] (Paris: La Fabrique, 2007), p. 89.

On the morning of the 24th, 'the troops, who had bivouacked in the rain with their feet in the mud, their minds troubled and their bodies numb with cold, perceived with the first glimmers of dawn a bold and resolute multitude, flocking to the rues Saint-Martin, Rambuteau, Saint-Merry, du Temple and Saint-Denis, where barricades had been raised in several places.'[6] These troops would rapidly break up, and the only serious fighting took place around the watertower that stood at the southern corner of the place du Palais-Royal. This was of course the moment described by Bakunin, who had just arrived on foot from Belgium:

> This enormous city, the centre of European culture, had suddenly become a wild Caucasus. In each street, almost everywhere, barricades erected like mountains and rising to the rooftops; above these barricades, between stones and damaged buildings, like Georgians on their rooftops, workers in blouses, black with powder and armed to the teeth . . . And in the midst of this unbounded joy, this intoxication, all had become so gentle, so human, pleasant, honest, modest, polite, kind and intelligent, that such a thing can be seen only in France, and even here only in Paris.[7]

On the afternoon of the 24th, Louis-Philippe signed his abdication in favour of his son, and left for England. So ended the first phase of the revolution of 1848, 'the shortest and least bloody that the country had known', wrote Tocqueville. Certainly the shortest, but a revolution that would spread from Denmark to the Adriatic, from the Rhine to the Vistula, from Mecklenburg to Croatia.

---

6 Daniel Stern (comtesse d'Agoult), *Histoire de la révolution de 1848* (Paris: Librairie Internationale, 1850), p. 74.

7 Mikhail Bakunin, *Confessions* (Paris: PUF, 1974), pp. 79–80. Cited in Jean-Christophe Angaut, *La Liberté des peuples: Bakounine et les révolutions de 1848* (Paris: Atelier de création libertaire, 2009).

Chapter 8

The Barricade Exported to Europe: Spring 1848

There can be little doubt that the example of Paris was the detonator for the 'springtime of peoples' of 1848: correlations have been noted between the dates of the various insurrections and the time needed for the news to arrive from Paris by the new means of communication – train and telegraph.[1] But the Paris spark fell on a European ground that had already been largely prepared, and indeed the first in date of the revolutions of 1848 took place not in Paris, but in Palermo.

Sicily, united with the kingdom of Naples by the Congress of Vienna in 1815 to form the kingdom of the two Sicilies, had long been in a state of ferment against the Bourbon king, Ferdinand II. On 9 January 1848, a refrain circulated in Palermo: 'We, a people born free but reduced to chains and misery, shall we still wait to conquer our legitimate rights? To arms, sons of Sicily!' On 12 January, barricades appeared in the central quarter of Fieracvecchia, the most wretched in the city, erected and defended by the poor, peasants from the environing countryside, 'brigands' and a section of the liberal nobility. The army, rather than risking a difficult

---

1 Mark Traugott, *The Insurgent Barricade*, (Berkeley, CA: University of California Press, 2010: p. 130. For example, a single day for Brussels, three days for Mannheim, seven days for Budapest.

confrontation in the tortuous streets of the centre, decided to bombard the city from the fortress of Castellammare, but on 15 January the insurgents were the masters of Palermo. They demanded the restoration of the constitution of 1812 that had established a Sicilian parliament and government. By mid-February they controlled all of Sicily, except Syracuse and the fortress of Messina. The movement spread to the kingdom of Naples, and for a moment Ferdinand's throne seemed to hang in the balance; but discord between the increasingly radicalized peasants and *lazzaroni*, and the upper classes set on preserving the social order, would lead the Sicilian revolution to defeat. Troops sent from Naples regained control of the island. The bombardment of Messina, which lasted for three whole days, earned Ferdinand the nickname of 'King Bomba'.

The movements that shook the centre of Europe from March 1848 onward were not homogeneous. One might even say that they pulled in opposing directions. In the German states and in Italy the dominant desire was national unity, whereas in the Habsburg Empire it was on the contrary a desire for secession or independence that shook Hungary and Bohemia. In places where radical networks had developed, the demand was for democratic freedoms, universal suffrage, the arming of the people, and even – as in the Rhineland regions of Germany, which had experienced for twenty years the influence of the French Revolution – a republic. In Cologne, news of the fall of Louis-Philippe was greeted by the *Marseillaise*. Where there were the beginnings of an industrial revolution – in Berlin or Vienna – the demands of workers and students were inspired by socialist doctrines,[2] while in the broad agricultural areas peasants demanded the abolition of feudal rights and land reform.

This great diversity, however, did not mean incoherence, and the accepted term of the 'springtime of peoples' is justified by the many

---

2   Marx and Engels published the *Communist Manifesto* in February – though with little resonance at first.

common features between the various revolts: hatred of absolutism and the European system established by the Congress of Vienna, as well as the quasi-general diffusion of a procedure that represented both a symbolic form and a military disposition: the barricade.

The term 'export' used in the title of this chapter is not arbitrary: its agents were the tens of thousands of political refugees in Paris – Italians, Hungarians, Poles and Germans. They returned to their home countries in the earliest days of the movement, and explained the mode of construction and use of the barricade which they had learned from their Paris comrades.

It would be long and cumbersome to relate each of the many revolutionary episodes that flared up in the kingdoms, grand duchies, free cities, provinces and other principalities of central Europe and Italy, so we shall limit ourselves here to the few generally regarded as essential.

Berlin, capital of the kingdom of Prussia, had become an industrial metropolis in the course of the 1840s, and was badly affected by an economic crisis in 1846–47. In March 1848, just as news came of the revolution in Paris, the Borsig locomotive factories dismissed a mass of workers, which triggered great tension among the working population. The Berliners assembled in the Tiergarten, the city's great central park, demanding a constitution and the creation of a ministry of labour.[3] They were dispersed by mounted police, and the first barricade was erected in Grünstrasse near the Rathaus, the Berlin town hall. On 16 March, when news came of the revolution in Vienna and the flight of Metternich, the insurrection spread throughout the city centre, where the main streets were blocked by barricades. On the night of the 18th, Friedrich-Wilhelm IV announced the abolition of censorship and the formation of a new ministry, as well as promising a constitution in the near future.

But the population's hatred of the army, combined with the court's spirit of revenge, made a peaceful end to absolutism impossible. An

3   Traugott, *Insurgent Barricade*, p. 134.

enormous crowd, informed of the king's concessions and gathered to acclaim him, discovered a mass of soldiers stationed in the courtyard of the castle, and noisily demanded their withdrawal. General von Prittwitz, the Berlin governor, gave the order to evacuate the area, but as in Paris in February on the boulevard des Capucines, guns were fired, the mêlée became general, and the battle spread to hundreds of barricades throughout the city, with more than two hundred dead on the insurgents' side. On the 19th the king gave way, ordering the withdrawal of the troops and placing himself under the protection of a civic guard. In a supreme humiliation, he was forced to salute the long convoy of victims of the violence, accompanied by the queen. On 21 March he announced in a grandiloquent proclamation 'to my people and the German nation' his intention to lead Germany towards unity and freedom, but the army that had withdrawn was still intact, a fact that weighed heavily on the subsequent course of events.

During this time (a necessary formula for days in which overlapping events unfolded in such a rush), students in Vienna were the first to react to the news from Paris. On 13 March, mingling with workers, they massed in the courtyard of the Landhaus, where a meeting of the estates of Lower Austria was to be held. The reading of a speech delivered a few days earlier to the Hungarian diet by Lajos Kossuth aroused enthusiasm: the crowd demanded a constitution and the departure of Metternich. But the troops were ordered to clear the square, leading to a confrontation in which several students were killed. The narrow streets of the old city were soon bristling with barricades, and the workers' districts rose up in turn. The aged Metternich, abandoned by the most influential members of the court, who advised him against continuing the repression, resigned and fled to England. On 15 March, Emperor Ferdinand I granted press freedom and the formation of a national guard, as well as promising to call a constituent assembly.

These unprecedented events provoked a shock wave across the whole Habsburg Empire. In Prague, Marshal Windischgrätz was initially overwhelmed by the student revolt inspired by the Viennese example. In Budapest, barricades forced the authorities to permit the establishment of a citizens' militia and the formation of a new executive, which the students called a 'committee of public safety'.[4] In Venice, news of the flight of Metternich triggered a revolt against the hated Austrians: the popular leaders Daniele Manin and Niccolò Tommaseo were liberated from prison, barricades went up throughout the city, the arsenal was stormed and arms distributed to the population. A republic was proclaimed – of which Manin would be president for nearly a year. In Milan, after five days of fighting on the barricades, the Austrian army commanded by Radetzky withdrew to Lodi and Mantua.

By the end of March 1848, the popular movement – and its barricade – seemed therefore to have triumphed in Germany and the Austrian empire. But everywhere, as we saw, the armies of absolutism withdrew before the movement without having been weakened. From the month of May onward – and above all after the crushing of the Paris proletariat in June – reaction would strike despite the efforts of the German parliament, assembled in Frankfurt, to prevent it. Windischgrätz restored order in Vienna and bombarded Prague, Friedrich-Wilhelm succeeded in reversing one by one the achievements of the March revolution, Habsburg imperial authority was gradually re-established in northern Italy, and the democratic regimes that had emerged throughout the peninsula were defeated one by one. By the end of 1848, the absolutist order had been restored almost everywhere.

However, amidst this general retreat the year 1849 still had a number of surprises in store. One of these episodes has remained famous, not so much on account of its political importance but rather because of the

4   Ibid., p. 139.

Barricades in Prague, June 1848

participation of two major figures, Richard Wagner and Mikhail
Bakunin. In Dresden, capital of the kingdom of Saxony, Friedrich-
August dissolved the chamber he had been forced to accept and called
on the Prussian army to help defeat the liberal opposition. In response
to this news, on 3 May 1849, Dresden was covered with barricades.

A few weeks before, Wagner, musical director of the Dresden royal opera, had conducted Beethoven's Ninth Symphony:

> Everyone did his utmost to make this one of the finest performances, and the public took up the matter with real enthusiasm. Michael Bakunin, unknown to the police, had been present at the public rehearsal. At its close he walked unhesitatingly up to me in the orchestra, and said in a loud voice, that if all the music that had ever been written were lost in the expected worldwide conflagration, we must pledge ourselves to rescue this symphony, even at the peril of our lives. Not many weeks after this performance it really seemed as though this worldwide conflagration would actually be kindled in the streets of Dresden, and that Bakunin, with whom I had meanwhile become more closely associated through strange and unusual circumstances, would undertake the office of chief stoker.[5]

The Prussian troops were preparing to attack:

> The Old Town of Dresden, with its barricades, was an interesting enough sight for the spectators. I looked on with amazement and disgust, but my attention was suddenly distracted by seeing Bakunin emerge from his hiding-place and wander among the barricades in a black frockcoat. But I was very much mistaken in thinking he would be pleased with what he saw; he recognized the childish inefficiency of all the measures that had been taken for defence, and declared that the only satisfaction he could feel in the state of affairs was that he need not trouble about the police, but could calmly consider the question of going elsewhere . . .

---

5   Richard Wagner, *My Life* (Rockville, MD: Wildside Press, 2010), p. 466.

On Sunday, 7 May, Wagner was at the top of the Kreuz tower that dominated the city:

> A sacred calm and peacefulness lay over the town and the wide suburbs of Dresden, which were visible from my point of vantage. Towards sunrise a mist settled upon the outskirts, and suddenly through its folds we could hear the music of the *Marseillaise* . . . As the sound drew nearer and nearer, the mist dispersed, and the glow of the rising sun spread a glittering light upon the weapons of a long column which was winding its way towards the town. . . . Here I beheld some thousand men from the Erzgebirge, mostly miners, well armed and organized, who had rallied to the defence of Dresden.[6]

But this support would not be sufficient:

> In the Town Hall I learned from Bakunin that the provisional government had passed a resolution, on his advice, to abandon the position in Dresden, which had been entirely neglected from the beginning, and was consequently quite untenable for any length of time. This resolution proposed an armed retreat to the Erzgebirge, where it would be possible to concentrate the reinforcement pouring in from all sides, especially from Thuringia, in such strength, that the advantageous position could be used to inaugurate a German civil war that would sound no hesitating note at its outset. To persist in defending isolated barricaded streets in Dresden could, on the other hand, lend little but the character of an urban riot to the contest, although it was pursued with the highest courage.[7]

---

6   Ibid., p. 484.
7   Ibid., pp. 487–8.

'I must confess', Wagner concludes, 'that this idea seemed to me magnificent and full of meaning.' With the help of Lizst, he managed to leave Saxony and reach Paris by way of Switzerland.

> Above all, the Void prevails; to scour
> Our history, laws and our rights; to devour
> Our sons' future life and our fathers' old bones,
> The beasts of the night creep from under their stones;
> Sophists and ruffians tighten their net;
> Radetzky is sniffing the muzzle's gibbet,
> Guilay, in tiger pelt, Buol green-faced,
> Haynau and Bomba prowl round, mouths agape,
> Around humankind and they, pale and enmeshed,
> Struggle for justice and for truthfulness;
> From Paris to Budapest, Rome to the East
> Over our bloody debris crawl these centipedes.[8]

8　Victor Hugo, *The Chastisements*, trans. by Adam Roberts, translatinghugo. blogspot.com.

Chapter 9

The Barricades of Despair: Paris, June 1848

It was in February 1848 in Paris that the last truly victorious barricades would be erected. After this date, all urban battles in which the insurrection based its tactics on barricades would be defeated, except for the ephemeral successes of spring 1848 elsewhere in Europe.

Despite this, the barricades of June 1848 are a moment unequalled in history – and not only the history of the barricade. Tocqueville described the June insurrection as

> the greatest and the strangest that had ever taken place in our history, or perhaps in that of any other nation: the greatest because for four days more than a hundred thousand men took part in it, and there were five generals killed; the strangest, because the insurgents were fighting without a battle cry, leaders, or flag, and yet they showed wonderful powers of coordination and a military expertise that astonished the most experienced officers.[1]

Another unique trait was that the June insurrection was conducted by the Paris proletariat alone: on the barricades this time were none of the students, artists and bohemians whose presence would be so

---

1 Alexis de Tocqueville, *Recollections*, (London: Macdonald, 1970) p. 136.

important for the Commune of 1871.[2] A few names stand out among
the leaders on the barricades, poor men's names, rescued from whole-
sale oblivion: Legénissel, an industrial draughtsman, Voisambert, a
shoe-mender, Barthélemy, a mechanic, Marche, a worker on the Nord
railway, Racary, also a mechanic, Hibruit, a hat-maker, Lahr and
Daix, builders.[3] Tocqueville was not mistaken: 'In truth it was not a
political struggle (in the sense in which we have used the word "political" up to now), but a class struggle, a sort of "Servile War".'[4]

Everything hinged on the question of the National Workshops.
After the February revolution, under popular pressure, a commission tasked with improving the lot of the workers had been formed,
based in the Luxembourg palace. 'On the proposal of M. Marie,
minister of public works, national workshops were hastily opened,
in which a tremendous number of workers were enrolled'[5] −
'tremendous' corresponding to the numbers of the unemployed.
Since there were not enough projects to occupy so many (over
100,000), the workshops became, in Marie's own words, 'organized
alms'. Workers were paid two francs for each working day, and one
franc if there was no work for them. As one of their number
explained, 'the Provisional Government gave the workshops a military organization' into platoons, companies and sections.[6] Perhaps
this was one reason for the amazing effectiveness of the Paris workers on the forthcoming barricades.

---

2   Among the rare exceptions were François Pardigon, a law student who
related his June adventures in *Épisodes des journées de juin 1848* (Paris: La Fabrique,
2008). Baudelaire took part in the February insurrection, but his presence on the
June barricades is unlikely.

3   See Victor Marouk, *Juin 1848* [1877] (Paris: Spartacus, 1998).

4   Tocqueville, *Recollections*, p. 136.

5   Louis Ménard, *Prologue d'une révolution*, [1848] (Paris: La Fabrique, 2007) p. 123.

6   Gustave Lefrançais, *Souvenirs d'un révolutionnaire* [1886] (Paris: Éditions
Tête de feuilles, 1972), p. 46.

Between February and May 1848, the ferment steadily grew. Clubs in Paris proliferated: the one with the largest membership, frequented also by respectable society, was Blanqui's club, the Société Républicaine Centrale, which met in the Salle du Conservatoire. In April, elections brought in a Constituent Assembly dominated by royalists and right-wing republicans, 'some priests and bishops, and lastly, a large number of generals, given the innate penchant of the French mind for military decorations: above all, there were landlords and capitalists'.[7] Against this background of tension, the Assembly was invaded on 15 May in the course of a popular demonstration in favour of Poland, leading to great disorder. Raspail and Blanqui (who had advised against the demonstration) addressed the assembly, but in the end the hall was cleared and the leaders of the democratic current were punished. Barbès, Albert and Raspail were imprisoned at Vincennes; Blanqui had managed to escape, but was arrested a few days later. On that day the proletariat lost all its natural leaders.

Both sides now prepared for a confrontation that each felt to be inevitable. Tocqueville, elected as deputy for Valognes, later wrote: 'The National Assembly was so constantly possessed by this thought that one might have said that it read the words "Civil War" written on the four walls of the House.'[8] Lamartine said to the Executive Commission (which had replaced the Provisional Government but resembled it like a twin):

> I demand two things; laws of public security respecting the rioters, the clubs, the abuses of complaint in anarchical journals, the power of banishing from Paris to their communes the agitators convicted of public sedition, and lastly a camp of twenty thousand men, under the walls of Paris, to assist the army of Paris and the National Guard

7   Ménard, *Prologue d'une révolution*, p. 150.

8   Tocqueville, *Recollections*, p. 136.

in the certain and imminent campaign which we would inevitably have to make against the National Workshops, and against the more guilty factions which might arise and become masters of this army of all the seditions.[9]

The Party of Order hastened to recruit a force designed to repress the popular movement: the Garde Mobile was formed of very young men, many of whom were working-class unemployed, attracted by the pay of thirty sous a day and the uniform. Their loyalty to the government, or rather the possibility of their going over to the insurrection, was of particular concern to Tocqueville: 'The various exclamations which we could hear from the battalions of the Garde Mobile [as they passed on review on the Champ-de-Mars] left us full of doubts and anxiety about the intentions of these young men, or rather children, who, more than anybody else at that time, held our destinies in their hands.'[10]

The workers also prepared for battle. Improvised powder workshops were constructed in the faubourg Saint-Antoine. Bullets were founded in sewing thimbles, and in the faubourg du Temple even a cannon was built.

On 21 June, the Executive Commission decided to put an end to the National Workshops. It decreed that workers aged between eighteen and twenty-five would be immediately enlisted in the army, and the rest would be sent to various departments to carry out earthworks. The first contingent was to leave Paris in two days' time, to drain the Sologne marshes.

At the news of this decree, on 22 June thousands of workers took to the streets, shouting: 'Down with Marie! Down with Lamartine! We're not leaving, we're not leaving!' A delegation led by Pujol, a

---

9   Alphonse de Lamartine, *Histoire de la révolution de 1848*, quoted in Eric Hazan, *The Invention of Paris* (London: Verso, 2010), p. 269.

10   Tocqueville, *Recollections*, p. 136.

lieutenant in the National Workshops, went to the Luxembourg to protest directly to Marie, who remained unmoved and finally uttered the fatal words: 'If the workers do not want to leave, we shall make them leave by force.' In the evening, a great crowd from all the workers' quarters, the 'famished masses' in Lamartine's words, converged on the place du Panthéon, where Workshops employees received their daily pay. Pardigon, one of the very few students to take part in the insurrection, explains:

> At certain moments, low murmurs and stirrings among these groups, in which even faces could not distinguished, showed that all minds were moved by a single thought, a thought as cold and severe as it was passionate . . . The spectre of the Sologne was present in everyone's mind, like a French Siberia to which the workers of the National Workshops were to be exiled, thus putting an end to the question of the Right to Work and ridding Paris of its revolutionary forces.[11]

On the night of 22–23 June, workers built barricades at three insurrectionary hubs. The first of these was on the slopes of Sainte-Geneviève, in the alleys around the Saint-Séverin church, on the Petit-Pont and in the warren of the Île de la Cité; the second was to the north, at the Poissonnière and Saint-Denis barriers [now Barbès and La Chapelle], attracting numerous railway mechanics; the third was in the faubourg Saint-Antoine and the faubourg du Temple, around the church of Saint-Gervais.

> In all the little streets around that building [the Hôtel de Ville] I found the people busy constructing barricades. They went about the work with the methodical skill of engineers, not taking up more paving-stones than were needed to provide squared stones for a

---

11   Pardigon, *Épisodes des journées de juin 1848*, p. 130.

solid and even fairly tidy wall, and they usually left a narrow opening by the houses to allow people to circulate.[12]

On the morning of the 23rd, accordingly, a line running from the
Panthéon to Barbès marked out the eastern half of Paris, which fell
into the hands of the insurrection without a shot having been fired.

The Executive Commission entrusted full military powers to
General Cavaignac, the minister of war. 'I am charged with crushing
the enemy and I shall act ruthlessly against him, as though at war.'
His troops were assembled on three spots: around the Porte Saint-
Denis under the command of Lamoricière, around the Hôtel de Ville,
and around the Sorbonne.

The fighting began at the Porte Saint-Denis, late in the morning
of the 23rd. The rue and the faubourg Saint-Denis, the rues
d'Aboukir and de Cléry, were filled with barricades. The highest of
these blocked the boulevard by the city gate. The detachment of
National Guards who arrived from the Madeleine was repelled, but
reinforcements were soon brought, and the leader of the barricade
was killed:

> A woman took up the flag; with thin hair and bare arms, she seemed
> to defy death. On seeing her, the National Guard hesitated to fire;
> they shouted to the young woman to get back; she remained
> undaunted, and provoked the attackers with her gestures and voice:
> a shot was fired, and she staggered and collapsed. But another
> woman suddenly rushed to her side; with one hand she supported
> the bloody body of her friend, with the other she hurled stones at
> the attackers. A new volley of shots echoed, and she fell in her turn
> on to the body that she was embracing.[13]

---

12   Tocqueville, *Recollections*, p. 138.
13   Stern (comtesse d'Agoult), *Histoire de la révolution de 1848*, p. 434.

A column of Gardes Mobiles and troops of the line, led by Lamoricière, arrived on the boulevard, stormed the barricade and swept everything away before them. But when the column turned north, towards the faubourg Poissonnière, it came up against the enormous defences on the place Lafayette commanded by Legénissel, a captain of the National Guard whose company had gone over to the insurrection. Lamoricière had to withdraw to the Porte Saint-Denis.

On the Left Bank, the troops massed at the Hôtel de Ville set off to attack the Montagne Saint-Geneviève by way of the Pont d'Arcole and the Pont Notre-Dame. The barricade defending the entrance to the rue Saint-Jacques held out for a long time, but on the arrival of the Mobile Guard it gave way.

The insurgents sought refuge in a draper's shop with the sign of Les Deux Pierrots, on the corner of the quay: their sad fate was to be massacred between the bales of cloth and the counters. But when the troops attacked on the rue Saint-Jacques, they were met by fire from every window, suffering enormous losses at one of the barricades that was built with a tiered structure. By nightfall there was no longer any question of reaching the Panthéon, and General Bedeau, who had taken a bullet in the thigh, ordered a withdrawal to the Hôtel de Ville.

There the situation was no better for the forces of order. Barricades surrounded the building on all sides, from the Cité, the rue Saint-Antoine, the rue du Temple, the alleys around the Saint-Gervais church. Between the place de l'Hôtel-de-Ville and the place du Châtelet, the troops were harassed by fire from the windows. Not long afterwards the insurgents took the town hall, winning a decisive moral advantage.

And so, on the evening of the 23rd, the first day of the June battle, the insurgents had secured their positions and were masters of half of Paris. But they lacked the unified command that would have enabled them to attack the other half, to launch an offensive against the Tuileries, the National Assembly, the Bank of France ... 'The leaders of the Democratic party had no hand in the insurrection. The most clever and energetic were [imprisoned] at Vincennes. The others lacked energy and faith; hence, among the popular party, this lack of unity, of an overall plan, which made possible the victory of their opponents.'[14]

That evening, the atmosphere in the Assembly was more than tense. Cavaignac, 'in a hoarse and jerky voice' as Tocqueville recalled, 'said that he had given orders to all the regiments posted along the railways to converge on Paris'.[15] It was decided that sixty deputies would go to shore up the morale of the forces of order, whose discouragement or even defection was feared. The envoys included two major witnesses of the events, Tocqueville and Victor Hugo. Hugo, for his part, emphasized his role as mediator, his concern to avoid a massacre. On the boulevard du Temple,

> The troops and mobiles lined the roofs of the boulevard du Temple and returned the fire of the insurgents. A cannon had just been drawn up in front of the Gaîté to demolish the house of the Galiote and sweep the whole boulevard. I thought I ought to make an effort to put a stop to the bloodshed, if possible, and advanced to the corner of the rue d'Angoulême [now Jean-Pierre-Timbaud]. As I was about to pass the little turret near there I was greeted with a fusillade. The turret was riddled with bullets behind me.[16]

The battle recommenced at dawn on the 24th. On the Left Bank, the troops attacked around the Saint-Séverin church and the place Maubert, and one by one removed the barricades on the rue Saint-Jacques. On reaching the top they came up against the large barricade built between the Panthéon and the Sainte-Geneviève library. An

---

14   Ménard, *Prologue d'une révolution*, p. 218.

15   Tocqueville, *Recollections*, p. 141.

16   Victor Hugo, *Things Seen* (Oxford: OUP, 1964), p. 232.

artillery battery was firing from the rue Soufflot, bullets crossed the nave of the Panthéon; soldiers managed to enter the law faculty building by a back door and shot at the insurgents there, who responded from the dome and the adjacent *mairie*. General Damesme, who had replaced Bedeau, was also wounded; he would die a few days later. But finally the door of the Panthéon gave way, the attack was launched, there was hand-to-hand fighting in the building, prisoners were shot on the spot, and the whole Montagne Sainte-Geneviève fell into the hands of the forces of order.

Towards the Hôtel de Ville and in the northern faubourgs, the barricades withstood the attack. Two generals, Korte and Bourgon, were killed in front of the defences of the place Lafayette, though ultimately these were overrun. The workers retreated to the Clos Saint-Lazare and the building site of the Hôpital du Nord [now Lariboisière].

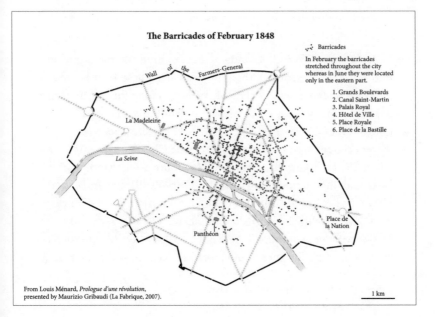

The Barricades of February 1848

Barricades

In February the barricades stretched throughout the city whereas in June they were located only in the eastern part.

1. Grands Boulevards
2. Canal Saint-Martin
3. Palais Royal
4. Hôtel de Ville
5. Place Royale
6. Place de la Bastille

Wall of the Farmers-General

La Madeleine

La Seine

Panthéon

Place de la Nation

From Louis Ménard, *Prologue d'une révolution*, presented by Maurizio Gribaudi (La Fabrique, 2007).

1 km

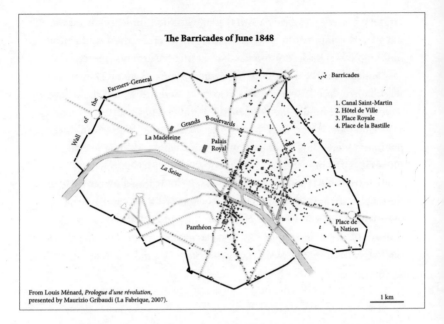

The Barricades of June 1848

· Barricades

1. Canal Saint-Martin
2. Hôtel de Ville
3. Place Royale
4. Place de la Bastille

Farmers-General

Wall of the

Grands Boulevards

La Madeleine

Palais Royal

La Seine

Panthéon

Place de la Nation

From Louis Ménard, *Prologue d'une révolution*, presented by Maurizio Gribaudi (La Fabrique, 2007).

1 km

On Sunday 25th, thousands of men poured off the trains and into Paris, in support of the government. 'These men belonged indiscriminately to every class of society; among them were many peasants, many shopkeepers, many landlords and nobles, all mingled together in the same ranks.'[17] The insurgents were steadily reduced to three sites of resistance: the Clos Saint-Lazare in the north, the faubourg du Temple and faubourg Saint-Antoine in the east, and the surroundings of the barrière d'Italie [now place d'Italie] in the south. Battles continued to rage, but the workers were overwhelmed by greater numbers. On the 26th only the faubourg Saint-Antoine still held out. A column led by Lamoricière arrived through the rues Popincourt and Basfroi, while the troops

---

17   Tocqueville, *Recollections*, p. 152.

massed at the Bastille swarmed into the faubourg with a formidable artillery. The battle was of short duration but dreadful violence. At ten in the morning, the insurgents capitulated. Sénard, the president of the Assembly, exclaimed: 'It's all over, gentlemen, thank God!'

The repression was ferocious. Workers caught with weapons were shot on the spot; others were taken to police stations, barracks and the Luxembourg palace, which were turned into slaughter-houses. Witnesses spoke of rivers of blood, heaped bodies, manhunts and cold-blooded slaughter. The dead, at least 10,000, were thrown into the Seine, dumped in wells, or buried in mass graves.

Blanqui, who as noted was in prison during those days, drew the lessons of the defeat in his *Instructions pour une prise d'armes*, written in 1861. He castigated the Parisian barricade:

> No point of leadership or overall command, not even consultation between the fighters. Each barricade has its particular group, more or less numerous but always isolated . . . Often there is not even a leader to direct the defence. The fighters just do what they like. They remain, they leave, they return, as they see fit. At night they go home to sleep. . . . 'Let each defend his post, and all will be well', the most solid ones say. This singular reasoning derives from the fact that the majority of insurgents fight in their own quarter, a capital error with disastrous consequences after defeat, especially in terms of denunciation by neighbours. For, with such a system, defeat is inevitable.[18]

In June, the lack of a general command that Blanqui denounced led to a defensive battle of barricades. By this stage, however, such a battle could only be lost, since no barricade could withstand artillery

---

18 Auguste Blanqui, *Maintenant il faut des armes*, ed. Dominique Le Nuz (Paris: La Fabrique, 2006), p. 259.

fire. Most importantly, the military leaders had learned the lessons of past blunders. No longer engaging their troops in isolated skirmishes where they risked being contaminated by the insurrection, they launched massive operations in which any fraternization could be ruled out. As Blanqui put it, 'while the insurgents smoked their pipes behind the paving-stones, the enemy successively concentrated all its forces on one point, then a second, a third, a fourth, and in this way exterminated the insurrection piece by piece.'

The June defeat was a dismal one, not least because few could afterwards be found to defend it and illustrate the heroism of the Paris workers. The only monograph on the subject, if I am not mistaken, dates from 1880. The reason for this silence is undoubtedly that 'on the side of the Paris proletariat there stood no one but itself'.[19] Those days were evoked above all by writers and poets, such as Baudelaire in his projected epilogue to *Les Fleurs du mal*:

> Your principles saved and laws decried,
> Your haughty monuments wrapped by mists,
> Your metal domes fired by the sun,
> Your theatre queens with enchanting voices,
> Your bells, cannons, deafening orchestra,
> Your magic cobbles erected into fortresses,
> Your little orators with baroque turns of phrase
> Preaching love, and then your sewers full with blood,
> Pouring into hell like so many Orinocos.[20]

---

19   Karl Marx, 'The Eighteenth Brumaire of Louis Bonaparte', in *Surveys from Exile* (London: Verso, 2011), p. 154.

20   Baudelaire, Projet d'épilogue pour *Les Fleurs du mal*, édition de 1861 (Paris: Gallimard, 1951), p. 210.

Barricade on the rue Saint-Maur before the attack by the forces of General
Lamoricière, Sunday, 25 June 1848

Barricade on the rue Saint-Maur after the attack by the forces of General
Lamoricière, Monday, 26 June 1848

Chapter 10

A Mythical Barricade: December 1851

After the massacres of June 1848, after the election of Louis Bonaparte as president of the republic in December the same year, after
the pitiful unarmed insurrection of the republicans of the 'Montagne'
in June 1849, the Second Republic slowly slipped towards the abyss.
The Legislative Assembly, dominated by the Party of Order –
Thiers, Montalembert, Falloux, Molé, Berryer – went so far as to
abolish universal suffrage on 31 May 1850. In order to register on the
electoral roll it was now necessary to prove one's residence in the
commune for three years, and proof of domicile was based on
'inscription on the personal tax roll', thus excluding a third of the
electoral body – what Thiers called 'the dangerous part of the great
agglomerations of population'. 'Faced with the flagrant advances of
socialism', Montalembert asked, 'shall we remain helpless and silent?'
Was it not the duty of all honest people 'to bring about that state of
affairs which the president of the republic defined so well when he
said that "The bad must tremble and the good be reassured"?'[1]

During the year 1851, the foremost issue was the revision of the
constitution to allow Louis Bonaparte to stand for the presidential election of May 1852 – a vital concern for him, given the level of his debts.

---

1   Cited in Henri Guillemin, *Le Coup du 2 décembre* (Paris: Gallimard, 1951),
p. 210.

Now imagine the French bourgeois, imagine how in the midst of this business his trade-crazy brain is tortured, whirled around and stunned by rumours of a coup d'état, by rumours that universal suffrage will be restored, by the struggle between parliament and the executive, by the Fronde-like war between Orleanists and Legitimists, by the communist conspiracies in southern France, by alleged *jacqueries* in the departments of Nièvre and Cher, by the publicity campaigns of the various presidential candidates, by the cheap and showy slogans of the newspapers, by the threats of the republicans to uphold the Constitution and universal suffrage by force of arms, by the preaching of the émigré heroes *in partibus*, who announced that the world would come to an end on the second Sunday in May 1852 – think of all this, and you will understand why the bourgeois, in this unspeakable, clamorous chaos of fusion, revision, prorogation, constitution, conspiration, coalition, emigration, usurpation and revolution, madly snorts at this parliamentary republic: *Rather an end with terror than terror without end.*

Bonaparte understood this cry.[2]

The coup d'état was launched on the night of 1–2 December, with the arrest of the potential leaders of a resistance:

It was a question of arresting at their own homes seventy-eight Democrats who were influential in their districts, and dreaded by the Élysée as possible chieftains of barricades. It was necessary, a still more daring outrage, to arrest at their houses sixteen Representatives of the People. For this last task were chosen among the Commissaries of Police such of those magistrates who seemed the most likely to become ruffians.[3]

---

2   Karl Marx, 'The Eighteenth Brumaire of Louis Bonaparte', in *Surveys from Exile* (London: Verso, 2011), pp. 227–8.

3   Victor Hugo, *History of a Crime* (New York: Mondial, 2005), p. 11. Hugo's

During the same night, the workers at the Imprimerie Nationale were engaged in the greatest secrecy in printing posters announcing the coup d'état. 'Each [of the compositors] was placed between two gendarmes, and forbidden to utter a single word, and then the documents which had to be printed were distributed throughout the room, being cut up in very small pieces, so that an entire sentence could not be read by one workman.'[4] Early in the morning, the National Assembly was occupied by the troops.

The representatives of the Party of Order met in the town hall of the tenth arrondissement, in the rue de Grenelle, and declared the dismissal of the prince-president – his dismissal, rather than outlawing, which would have had more serious implications. 'Popular armed resistance, even in the name of the law, seemed sedition to them. The utmost appearance of revolution which they could endure was a regiment of the National Guard, with their drums at their head; they shrank from the barricade; Right in a blouse was no longer Right, Truth armed with a pike was no longer Truth, Law unpaving a street gave them the impression of a Fury.'[5] These 300-odd right-wing deputies would be taken to the Orsay barracks, then conveyed in prison carriages to Mazas and Mont Valérien: 'the entire Party of Order arrested in a body and taken to prison by the *sergents de ville*!'[6]

Meanwhile some sixty deputies of the left, including Edgar Quinet, Schoelcher, Carnot and Hugo himself, met in the apartment of a friend on the rue Blanche. Hugo proposed they should issue a proclamation:

'Dictate,' said Baudin to me, 'I will write.'
I dictated:

---

book, an incomparable account of the events of 2–4 December, is subtitled 'The Testimony of an Eye-Witness'.

4   Ibid., p. 13.
5   Ibid., p. 73.
6   Ibid., p. 83.

'TO THE PEOPLE.

Louis-Napoléon Bonaparte is a traitor.

He has violated the Constitution.

He is forsworn.

He is an outlaw . . .'[7]

They then decided to try to energise Paris, starting with the working-class districts. Hugo remembered Auguste, a wine merchant whose life he had saved in 1848: 'I thought that he might give me information about the faubourg St. Antoine, and help us in rousing the people.' Having with difficulty found Auguste's shop, on the rue de la Roquette, he entered:

He knew me at once, and came up to me.

'Ah, Sir,' said he, 'it is you!'

'Do you know what is going on?' I asked him.

'Yes, sir.'

This 'yes, sir', uttered with calmness, and even with a certain embarrassment, told me all. Where I expected an indignant outcry I found this peaceable answer. It seemed to me that I was speaking to the faubourg St. Antoine itself. I understood that all was at an end in this district, and that we had nothing to expect from it.

Auguste explained himself, and the indirect style Hugo uses here emphasises the sadness of his words:

To tell the whole truth, people did not care much for the Constitution, they liked the Republic, but the Republic was maintained too much by force for their taste. In all this they could only see one thing clearly, the cannon ready to slaughter them – they remembered June, 1848 – there were some poor people who had suffered

---

7   Ibid., p. 101.

greatly – Cavaignac had done much evil – women clung to the men's blouses to prevent them from going to the barricades – nevertheless, with all this, when seeing men like ourselves at their head, they would perhaps fight, but this hindered them, they did not know for what.[8]

In the evening of this first day of the coup d'état, the representatives of the republican left decided despite everything to try to rouse the faubourg Saint-Antoine. They agreed to meet at nine the next morning in the Salle Roysin, a large café that had been the meeting-place of the social-democratic club in 1848. 'Rebellion in the Élysée, the government in the faubourg Saint-Antoine!' Hugo exclaimed.

We have an eye-witness account of the events of that morning by a courageous participant, Victor Schoelcher.[9] On the way to the Salle Roysin,

proceeding on foot through the faubourg Saint-Antoine, we saw groups of workers gathered at the doors of their houses. They were dejected, but calm, and when we asked: 'Are you doing nothing? Are you waiting for the empire?' they all replied: 'No, no, never!', adding: 'What do you want us to do? We have no weapons, we were disarmed after June 1848!' These last words were repeated to us ten times by different groups. Oh, those who disarmed the people then were guilty of much! . . . Despite everything, the republican representatives,[10] with some twenty bold men in blouses and suits, decided on the first barricade erected against the

---

8   Ibid., pp. 111–12.

9   Victor Schoelcher, *Histoire des crimes du 2 décembre* (2 vols, Brussels, 1852). The quotations are taken from vol. 1, pp. 190–210.

10   'They were eight on the barricade: Baudin, Bruckner, Deflotte, Dulac, Maigne, Malardière, Schoelcher [who writes of himself in the third person], and another whom we cannot name because the prosecutors are unaware of him.'

ex-president's insurrection . . . We immediately set to work to make a barricade across the faubourg at the corners of the rues de Cotte and Sainte-Marguerite [now Trousseau]. A dairy cart, another baker's cart, a large wagon and an omnibus were successively seized, unhitched and turned upside down . . . We possessed only three rifles taken from two passing soldiers accompanied just by an old sergeant. From where we were we could see the small building of the Corps de garde in the middle of the faubourg Saint-Antoine, near the rue de Montreuil. We fell on this post and forced it to hand over its weapons, ten or twelve rifles, and its munitions. We then headed for the guard post of the Marché-Noir [now Aligre]. The same expedition, again led by deputies, was carried out with the same audacity and the same success.

A few minutes after we returned to the barricade, around half past nine, we noticed an infantry detachment of the 19th light regiment approaching from the direction of the Bastille. . . . When the detachment came close, one of us said to his colleagues: 'Let's move forward.' Immediately the representatives climbed on the overturned vehicles, and this man, addressing the citizens, said: 'Friends, not a shot before the troops open fire.' . . . The three companies proceeded silently at a funeral pace. We made a sign to them to halt; the captain at their head replied with a negative sign; seven [of us] then descended and advanced towards him. The captain threatened: 'Go back or I'll fire.' 'You can kill us,' the Montagnards replied with one voice, 'but you will not make us retreat; our bodies will serve to cover the people!'

They could have killed us, but they did not want to. They passed between us. Nine ranks of soldiers, coming towards the barricade, successively found themselves face to face with us; none of them struck. The troop loosed only one volley, and it was then that our colleague Baudin, who had remained standing fast on one of the vehicles, received three bullets in the head that killed him immediately. None of us, further forwards, saw him

fall. . . . The representative of the people Baudin will be inscribed
on the glorious and too long list of the martyrs of liberty. His
death was not without bitterness. 'We didn't want to sacrifice
ourselves for the "twenty-five francs",' one worker said. 'The
twenty-five francs'! That is what even some of our own friends
foolishly called us.[11] 'You shall see', Baudin replied, 'how someone dies for twenty-five francs!' And it was precisely he who laid
down his life for the Constitution, bequeathing to posterity his
name and a sublime phrase!

Hugo writes that the evening was full of menace. Groups formed
on the boulevards, soon combining into a tremendous crowd:

Throughout that long line from the Madeleine to the Bastille, the
roadway nearly everywhere, except (was this on purpose?) at

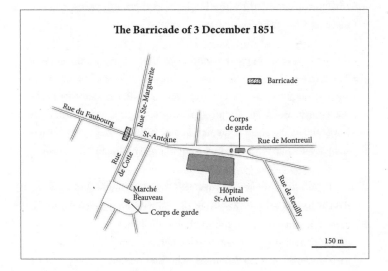

The Barricade of 3 December 1851

---

11   Under the Second Republic deputies received twenty-five francs a day.

the Porte St Denis and the Porte St Martin, was occupied by the soldiers – infantry and cavalry, ranged in battle-order, the artillery batteries being harnessed; on the pavements on each side of this motionless and gloomy mass, bristling with cannon, swords, and bayonets, flowed a torrent of angry people.[12]

Small barricades were erected in the old insurrectionary quarters, between the Hôtel de Ville and the boulevards. The fighters did not try to defend these at any cost, but rather used them to dodge the attacks of the troops, abandoning one position and taking up another. At the Élysée there was a certain disquiet. Morny, the new interior minister, himself redrafted a proclamation by Saint-Arnaud, the new minister of war, ending it with the words: 'Any individual taken constructing or defending a barricade, or with weapons in hand, will be shot.'[13]

On the morning of 4 December, barricades proliferated within a quadrilateral bounded by the Halles and the boulevards, the rue du Temple and the rue Montmartre.

At eleven o'clock in the morning from Notre-Dame to the Porte St Martin there were seventy-seven barricades. Three of them, one in the rue Maubuée, another in the rue Bertin-Poirée, another in the rue Guérin-Boisseau, attained the height of the second stories; the barricade of the Porte St Denis was almost as bristling and as formidable as the barrier of the faubourg Saint-Antoine in June, 1848.[14]

But the military chiefs had assembled some 30,000 men in the city centre, who moved into action in the afternoon. At two o'clock, five

---

12   Hugo, *History of a Crime*, p. 194.

13   Guillemin, *Le Coup du 2 décembre*, p. 386.

14   Hugo, *History of a Crime*, p. 265. The June barricade on the faubourg Saint-Antoine is described at length in book V of *Les Misérable*s.

brigades were positioned on the boulevards between the rue de la Paix and the faubourg Poissonnière:

> In the twinkling of an eye there was a butchery on the boulevard a quarter of a league long. Eleven pieces of cannon wrecked the Sallandrouze carpet warehouse. The shot tore completely through twenty-eight houses. The baths of Jouvence were riddled. There was a massacre at Tortoni's. A whole quarter of Paris was filled with an immense flying mass, and with a terrible cry. Everywhere sudden death. A man is expecting nothing. He falls.[15]

A terrifying blow had to be dealt. This explains the massacre of an unarmed crowd, the slaughter inside buildings, the deliberate carnage. 'On a given signal,' wrote Odilon Barrot in his *Mémoires*, 'columns of infantry and cavalry rushed on the crowd. This murder was not a mistake, *a bit of terror was needed*, if only to expand the event.'[16]

Today this crime has been amnestied, so to speak, drowned in the rampant rehabilitation of Louis Bonaparte that has already been under way for years – witness the name of Napoléon III given to the esplanade in front of the Gare du Nord, or Philippe Séguin's book entitled *Louis Napoléon le Grand* (1990). The death of Baudin on the barricade has likewise been buried in a remote corner of collective memory; his statue was melted down under the Occupation, and the street that bears his name is one of the most dismal in the eleventh arrondissement.[17] Few remember that the name of Baudin was a weapon against the regime at the end of the empire, when in 1868, on

---

15   Ibid., p. 270.

16   Cited in Guillemin, *Le Coup du 2 décembre*, p. 398. My emphasis.

17   A plaque was however placed in 1879 on the building at no. 151, rue du Faubourg-Saint-Antoine.

the initiative of Charles Delescluze, a subscription was launched in the press to erect a monument to him – inspired by a planned trial of radical republicans for 'incitement to hatred and contempt for the government'.

Chapter 11

The Barricades of the Commune: May 1871

Seventy days elapsed between 18 March 1871, when the people of Paris seized the cannon of the National Guard in Montmartre, and 28 May, when the last shots were fired in Belleville. It was only in the final week that the barricade played a part, yet this is remembered as the symbol of the Paris Commune.

How did things get to such a pass, in that tragic week, when the Commune still possessed the assets of weapons, fortifications and cannon?[1]

A first reason is that the city of Paris very soon found itself alone in its struggle. The communes of Marseille, Narbonne and Limoges were subdued within days, enabling Thiers to concentrate his forces around the capital.

Another major reason was the friction within the Paris movement. The central committee of the National Guard, elected by the battalions of the popular quarters, was the revolutionary body that took possession of the city on 18 March. It would cede power to the Commune elected by universal suffrage, but without dissolving itself: it continued to play an ill-defined role, a factor of discord and

---

1 See Prosper-Olivier Lissagaray, *History of the Paris Commune of 1871* [1876] (London: Verso, 2012), an indispensable work, by a participant who spent the rest of his life studying the history of the events he had lived through.

confusion. The Commune itself was divided into two wings from its very first session. The majority was made up of 'Jacobins', haunted by the memory of 1793 – these included the great Charles Delescluze – along with Blanquists such as Eudes, Ferré, Rigault and Ranvier. These 'romantics', as Lissagaray called them, were republicans who favoured a centralist, authoritarian politics. The minority, for their part, were Internationals, Proudhonists or independents, champions of social democracy and hostile to republican centralization.[2] They included Courbet, Fränkel, Lefrançais, Longuet, Malon, Tridon (despite his being a follower of Blanqui), Vallès and Vermorel. Their opposition would become more fiery when, in the face of general disorganization, the majority decided on the formation of a Committee of Public Safety – which was far from working wonders.

When the Versaillais entered Paris, all these tendencies united to confront the danger, but it was too late: the defence was not ready. Successive delegates for war (the Commune did not have ministers) came and went without any of them showing signs of competence: Cluseret ('We must admit that the Commune possesses a delegate for war of great calm and with a remarkable power of sleep. Good heavens, what a sleeper!'[3]) was replaced by his chief of staff, Rossel, a professional soldier, 'absolutely foreign to the cause for which we struggle – how could that communion of ideas that is indispensable for success be established between his troops and himself?'[4] On the

---

2   In his *Enquête sur la Commune de Paris* published by the *Revue Blanche* in 1897, Lefrançais wrote: 'The twenty-five years that have passed since then have only convinced me more that this minority were right, and that the proletariat will never succeed in truly emancipating itself without ridding itself of the Republic, the last form of authoritarian government, and by no means the least harmful' (Gustave Le français, *Souvenirs d'un révolutionnaire*, new edition, [Paris: Éditions de l'Amateur, 2011], p. 105).

3   Lefrançais, *Souvenirs d'un révolutionnaire*, p. 389.

4   Ibid., p. 401.

brink of disaster, Delescluze was appointed delegate for war: a superb symbol, but the man himself was old, tired, ill, and ignorant of military matters. The Commune's army never had a real head, which was clearly a fatal lack.

A barricades commission was established in early April, under Rossel, an officer of the engineers. It decided to construct lines of barricades around the city. The idea was for barricade-fortresses on the main communication routes, and lighter constructions elsewhere.[5] Napoléon Gaillard, a master shoemaker, was charged by Rossel to undertake this work. In fact, only a few of the large barricades envisaged were in place to meet the Versaillais: the largest of these – the 'Château-Gaillard' – blocked the rues Saint-Florentin and Rivoli at the corner of the place de la Concorde. Others were erected at the Trocadéro, on the rue de Castiglione, and in the fourteenth arrondissement on the avenue de Maine at the Porte d'Orléans, but this was very far from being the second defensive wall originally planned. 'These were no longer the traditional redoubts two storeys high. Save four or five in the rue Saint-Honoré and the rue de Rivoli, the barricades of May consisted of a few paving-stones hardly a man's height; behind these sometimes a cannon or a machine-gun; and in the midst, wedged in by two paving-stones, the red flag, the colour of vengeance.'[6]

The vanguard of the Versaillais troops entered Paris in the early hours of 21 May, flooding in 'through the five gaping wounds of the gates of Passy, Auteuil, Saint-Cloud, Sèvres and Versailles. The greater part of the fifteenth arrondissement was occupied, the Muette taken; all Passy and the heights of the Trocadéro were taken.'[7] During this time, the general council of the Commune held

---

5 Marcel Cerf, 'La barricade de 1871', in Alain Corbin and Jean-Marie Mayeur, eds, La Barricade (Paris, Publications de la Sorbonne, 1997), pp. 323–35.

6 Lissagaray, *History of the Paris Commune*, p. 258.

7 Ibid., p. 248.

its last session in the Hôtel de Ville. It dealt only with regular business.

On the morning of 22 May, a proclamation written by Delescluze could be read on the walls:

> Enough of militarism! No more staff-officers with their gold-embroidered uniforms! Make way for the people, for the combatants bare-armed! The hour of the revolutionary war has struck . . . The people know nothing of learned manoeuvres. But when they have a gun in their hands and paving-stones under their feet, they fear not all the strategists of the monarchical school.[8]

In the words of Lefrançais, 'it was essential to put an end to this nightmare of interminable siege . . . Better for all, in sum, this definitive face-to-face than the indefinite continuation of a struggle at a distance and with no outcome. The invaders were awaited almost with impatience, on the heights of Passy and the Trocadéro that they had taken possession of during the night.'[9]

As it seemed impossible to mount a defence on the wide arteries of the west of the city, the Federals withdrew to a line running from the Batignolles to the Gare Montparnasse, via Saint-Augustin and Concorde. But this line soon collapsed, except at the Batignolles which formed a forward defence for Montmartre; here the Versaillais were stopped between the place Clichy and La Fourche. The Butte Montmartre, however, which could have been an impregnable fortress, remained silent. 'Eighty-five cannon and about twenty machine-guns were lying there, dirty, pell-mell, and no one during these eight weeks had even thought of cleaning them.' On the Left Bank, where the rue de l'Université, the rue du Bac and the boulevard Saint-Germain were barricaded, soldiers filed through the

---

8   Ibid., pp. 249–50.

9   Lefrançais, *Souvenirs d'un révolutionnaire*, p. 420.

avenue du Maine to the Gare Montparnasse. 'This position, of supreme importance, had been utterly neglected; about twenty men defended it, and they were soon short of cartridges, and obliged to retreat to the rue de Rennes, where, under the fire of the troops, they constructed a barricade at the top of the rue du Vieux Colombier.'[10]

By the evening of the 22nd, the Versaillais line stretched from the Gare des Batignolles to the Gare Montparnasse, by way of the Gare Saint-Lazare, Saint-Augustin, the Palais-Bourbon and the boulevard des Invalides. But 'Paris, the old insurgent, resumed her combative physiognomy. Dispatch riders dashed through the streets, and remainders of battalions came to the Hôtel de Ville, where the Central Committee, the Committee of Artillery, and all the military services were concentrated.'[11]

Early in the morning of the 23rd, the Versaillais launched a movement that skirted the fortifications and took all the northern gates from behind, from Asnières to Saint-Ouen – the Prussians had let them pass. The Batignolles barricades gave way one after the other. Columns attacked Montmartre through the rue Lepic and the rue Clignancourt. The Montmartre cemetery saw bitter fighting, with Louise Michel taking up a rifle: 'This time the shell fell close to me, coming down through the branches and covering me with flowers, close to Murger's tomb. . . . When I returned to my comrades, near the tomb on which stands the bronze statue of Cavaignac, they said to me: now keep still.'[12]

On the place Blanche, at the mouth of the rue Lepic, the famous women's barricade, commanded by the Russian revolutionary

---

10   Lissagaray, *History of the Paris Commune*, p. 253.

11   Ibid.

12   Louise Michel, *La Commune, histoire et souvenirs* [1898] (Paris: La Découverte, 1999), pp. 232–3. The Cavaignac she refers to here is Godefroy Cavaignac, one of the republican leaders under the July monarchy, who died of tuberculosis in 1845. The recumbent figure on his tomb was the work of Rude.

Elisabeth Dmitrieff and made up of militants from the Union des Femmes, held out for several hours while other women came to reinforce the barricade on place Pigalle, at the bottom of the rue Houdon.[13]

Resistance was more effective on the other bank of the Seine, particularly at the two crossroads of Croix-Rouge and Vavin, where Varlin managed to hold out for two days. He only abandoned this sector when fire and mortar shells had made it a field of ruins. Here again, however, the Versaillais, turning around to the south along the ramparts, came up through the avenue de Maine to the place d'Enfer [now Denfert-Rochereau]. On the Butte-aux-Cailles, Wroblewski, one of the best officers of the Polish insurrection of 1863, 'installed a battery of eight pieces and two batteries of four . . . a dominant position between the Panthéon and the forts; he fortified the boulevards d'Italie [now Auguste-Blanqui], de l'Hôpital, and de la Gare [now Vincent Auriol]. He established his headquarters at the mairie des Gobelins, with reserves at the place d'Italie, the place Jeanne d'Arc, and Bercy.'[14]

On the evening of 23 May, the Versaillais line extended from the Porte de la Chapelle to the place d'Enfer, by way of the Gare du Nord, the new Opéra, the boulevard des Italiens and the rue du Bac. 'The place de la Concorde and the rue Royale, surrounded on their flanks, stood out like a promontory in the midst of a tempest,' wrote Lissagaray. That evening the massacre of prisoners began, and of all those suspected of taking part in the insurrection. Each army corps had its provost marshal who ordered executions and, so as to proceed more quickly, supplementary provosts were posted in the conquered streets.

---

13   Alain Dalotel, 'La barricade des femmes' (in Corbin and Mayeur, eds, *La Barricade*, pp. 350–5), emphasises that there could be an element of legend in this episode.

14   Lissagaray, *History of the Paris Commune*, p. 263.

During the night the Tuileries burned. 'Formidable detonations were heard from the palace of the kings, whose walls were falling, its vast cupolas giving way. . . . The red tide of the Seine reflected the monuments, thus redoubling the conflagration.'[15] On the Left Bank, the Légion d'honneur building and the Cour des Comptes likewise went up in flames, so that 'the rue Royale to St Sulpice seemed a wall of fire divided by the Seine.'[16] At ten in the evening, the barricade in the rue Saint-Florentin was evacuated, the Versaillais occupied the place Vendôme and took the barricade on the rue de Castiglione from behind. The Federals withdrew with great difficulty to the Hôtel de Ville.

In the morning of 24th May, the Versaillais pushed forwards on all fronts. They cannonaded the Palais-Royal, reached the Bourse and descended towards the Halles, where they met very strong resistance around Sainte-Eustache. On the Left Bank, they reached the Val-de-Grâce and approached the Panthéon. At eight o'clock, members of the Commune met at the Hôtel de Ville and decided to evacuate it. The building was set on fire, and the services of the war department withdrew to the *mairie* of the eleventh arrondissement. What remained of the defence line was cut in two, and communication between the two banks became dangerous.

On the Left Bank, the Federals abandoned the rue Vavin, blowing up the powder works at the Luxembourg. Varlin and Lisbonne retreated to the Panthéon, defended by three barricades, the farther and higher one running between the *mairie* of the fifth arrondissement and the law faculty building. But the Versaillais surged across the Pont Saint-Michel, where firing had stopped for lack of munitions. In the afternoon, the Panthéon was taken and the whole of the Montagne Sainte-Geneviève fell into the hands of the army. The massacres immediately commenced: on the rue Saint-Jacques, forty prisoners were shot.

---

15 Ibid., p. 267.
16 Ibid.

At the *mairie* of the eleventh arrondissement, where the remnants of the battalions of the conquered quarters were gathered, it was Delescluze who spoke:

> 'I propose,' said he, 'that the members of the Commune, engirded with their scarfs, shall make a review of all the battalions that can be assembled on the boulevard Voltaire. We shall then at their head proceed to the points to be reconquered.' . . . Behold, in the midst of this defeat, this old man upright, his eyes luminous, his right hand raised defying despair, these armed men fresh from the battle suspending their breath to listen to this voice which seemed to ascend from the tomb. There was no scene more solemn in the thousand tragedies of that day.[17]

The defence of the east of Paris was organized. Around the Bastille, barricades defended the entry to the rue and faubourg Saint-Antoine. On the place du Château-d'Eau [now de la République], a wall of paving-stones blocked the entrance to the boulevard Voltaire. The rues Oberkampf, Angoulême, la Fontaine-au-Roi and Faubourg du Temple were hastily barricaded at their lower ends.

The massacre continued in the neighbourhoods occupied by the army. "These are no longer soldiers accomplishing a duty", said a conservative journal, *La France*. And indeed these were hyenas, thirsting for blood and pillage. In some places it sufficed to have a watch to be shot. The corpses were searched, and the correspondents of foreign newspapers called those thefts the last perquisition.'[18] In response the Federals executed Darboy, the archbishop of Paris, Deguerry, vicar of the Madeleine, and three Jesuits imprisoned with them in La Roquette.

---

17   Ibid., p. 275.
18   Ibid., p. 277.

Barricade on the rue d'Allemagne (now avenue Jean-Jaurès) at the
crossroads with the rue de Sébastopol (now rue Lally-Tollendal), 1871

On the night of the 24th, the Versaillais troops occupied a great
swath surrounding the eleventh, nineteenth and twentieth arrondissements, while Paris continued to burn.

At midday on the 25th, the army attacked the Butte-aux-
Cailles from the avenue d'Italie in the south and the Gobelins in
the north. 'For three hours a prolonged and obstinate firing
enveloped the Butte aux Cailles, battered down by the Versaillese
cannon, six times as numerous as Wroblewski's. . . . protected by
the fire of the Austerlitz Bridge, the able defender of the Butte
aux Cailles passed the Seine in good order with his cannon and a
thousand men.'[19] The whole of the Left Bank was now in the
hands of the Versaillais.

---

19   Ibid., pp. 283, 284.

The barricades defending the entrance to the boulevard Voltaire and the boulevard du Temple came under fire from the Prince-Eugène barracks [of the Republican Guard, on the place de la République], from the boulevard Magenta and the rue Turbigo. 'The place du Château d'Eau was ravaged as by a cyclone. The walls crumbled beneath the shells and bullets; enormous blocks were thrown up; the lions of the fountains perforated or broken off, the basin surmounting it shattered. Fire burst out from twenty houses. The trees were leafless, and their broken branches hung like limbs all but parted from the main body.'[20]

Delescluze came down the boulevard Voltaire towards the square. He wore

> his ordinary dress, black hat, coat, and trousers, his red scarf, incon-
> spicuous as was his wont, tied round his waist. Unarmed, he leant
> on a cane. . . . At about eighty yards from the barricade the guards
> who accompanied him kept back, for the projectiles obscured the
> entrance of the boulevard.
>
> Delescluze still walked forward. Behold the scene; we have witnessed
> it; let it be engraved in the annals of history. The sun was setting. The old
> exile, unmindful whether he was followed, still advanced at the same
> pace, the only living being on the road. Arrived at the barricade, he bent
> off to the left and mounted upon the paving-stones. For the last time his
> austere face, framed in his white beard, appeared to us turned towards
> death. Suddenly Delescluze disappeared. He had fallen as if thunder-
> stricken on the place du Château d'Eau.[21]

By the evening, only two whole arrondissements remained in the hands of the Commune, the nineteenth and twentieth, along with half of the eleventh.

---

20   Ibid., p. 287.
21   Ibid., pp. 287–8.

On the morning of Friday, 26 May, the fighting was concentrated on the Bastille, under attack from two sides, the boulevard Mazas [now Diderot] and the boulevard Beaumarchais:

> Entrenched in the houses, the Federals fell, but neither yielded nor retreated; and, thanks to their self-sacrifice, the Bastille for six hours still disputed its shattered barricades and ruined houses. . . . Leaning against the same wall the sons of the combatants of June fought for the same pavement as their fathers. . . . The house at the corner of the rue de la Roquette, the angle of the rue de Charenton, disappeared like the scenery of a theatre, and amidst these ruins, under these burning beams, some men fired their cannon, and ten times raised the red flag, ten times struck down by Versaillese fire.[22]

The Bastille succumbed at around two in the afternoon. There was still fighting at La Villette, around the Rotonde, the quai de Loire and the rue de Crimée. But a fire broke out on the docks, full of petroleum and explosives, and the barricade defenders had to retreat to the twentieth arrondissement.

It was on that evening of the 26th that the hostages were shot on the rue Haxo. These were thirty-four gendarmes captured at Belleville and Montmartre on 18 March, ten Jesuits, monks and priests, and four imperial spies. 'And yet for two days the soldiers taken prisoner passed through Belleville without exciting a murmur; but these gendarmes, these spies, these priests, who for fully twenty years had trampled upon Paris, represented the Empire, the bourgeoisie, the massacres under their most hateful forms.'[23]

On the morning of Saturday, 27 May, Jules Vallès was in the rue des Trois-Bornes: 'We stayed up all night. At dawn, Cournet, Theisz, Camélinat and myself went back towards Paris. The rue

---

22 Ibid., p. 292.
23 Ibid., p. 297.

d'Angoulême still held out. There, the 209th, the battalion whose standard-bearer was Camélinat, was desperately defending itself.'[24] The Versaillais occupied the Montreuil and Bagnolet gates, the place du Trône [now de la Nation], and spread from there into Charonne. From La Villette, their mortars devastated the Buttes-Chaumont. The artillery of the Federals, massed on the place des Fêtes, stopped firing in the afternoon for lack of munitions, and their gunners joined those defending the rue Fessart and the rue des Annelets:

> Since four o'clock in the afternoon the Versaillese had been laying siege to the Père Lachaise, which enclosed no more than 200 Federals, resolute, but without discipline or foresight. The officers had been unable to make them embattle the walls. Five thousand Versaillese approached the enceinte from all sides, while the artillery of the bastion furrowed the interior. . . . At six o'clock the Versaillese, not daring, in spite of their numbers, to scale the enceinte, cannonaded the large gate of the cemetery, which soon gave way, notwithstanding the barricade propping it up. Then began a desperate struggle. Sheltered behind the tombs, the Federals disputed their refuge foot by foot; . . . in the vaults they fought with sidearms. . . . The darkness that set in early did not end the despair.[25]

At five in the morning on Sunday, 28 May, 'we were at the giant barricade at the foot of the rue de Belleville, almost facing the Salle Favié,' wrote Vallès:

> I had drawn lots with the officer replacing me as to who would go and lie down for a while. It fell to me and I stretched out in an old bed at

---

24   Jules Vallès, *L'Insurgé* [1886] (Paris: G. Charpentier, 1908), p. 320. Camélinat, a sculptor in bronze and a member of the International, was head of the mint during the Commune.

25   Lissagaray, *History of the Paris Commune*, p. 300.

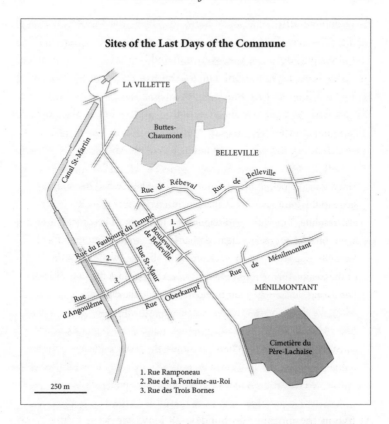

Sites of the Last Days of the Commune

1. Rue Ramponeau
2. Rue de la Fontaine-au-Roi
3. Rue des Trois Bornes

250 m

the back of an abandoned apartment. . . . We replied with rifles and cannon to the terrible fire directed against us. In the windows of La Veilleuse,[26] and of all the houses on the corner, our people had put straw mattresses whose stuffing was smouldering and punctured.[27]

---

26 This café still exists on the corner of the rue de Belleville and the boulevard de Belleville. The building has been recently reconstructed.

27 Vallès, *L'Insurgé*, pp. 321–2. The Salle Favié stood near the site of the present café Les Folies.

In the course of the morning the resistance was reduced to the small quadrilateral bounded by the rue du Faubourg-du-Temple, the rue Saint-Maur and the boulevard de Belleville.

Several streets today compete for the honour of having hosted the final barricade of the Commune. For Lissagaray, 'the last barricade of the May days was in the rue Ramponeau. For a quarter of an hour a single Federal defended it. Thrice he broke the staff of the Versaillese flag hoisted on the barricade of the rue de Paris [now de Belleville]. As a reward for his courage, this last soldier of the Commune succeeded in escaping.' Legend has it that this soldier was Lissagaray himself.

For others, the last barricade was that on the rue Rébeval; for Louise Michel it was that of the rue de la Fontaine-au-Roi:

> An immense red flag floated above the barricade. The two Ferrés were there, Théophile and Hippolyte, also J.-B. Clément, Cambon, a Garibaldian, Varlin, Vermorel, Champy. The barricade on the rue Saint-Maur had just succumbed, that of La Fontaine-au-Roi stubbornly spat out fire in the bloody face of Versailles. . . . At the moment when the last shots were fired, a young woman arrived from the barricade on the rue Saint-Maur, to offer her services. They tried to push her away from this place of death, but she stayed despite them.[28]

This was the woman to whom Jean-Baptiste Clément would dedicate his song, *Le Temps des cerises*.

At one o'clock, it was all over.

---

28   Michel, *La Commune*, p. 264.

Epilogue

Petrograd 1917, Berlin 1919, Barcelona 1936, Madrid 1937, Paris 1944: the first half of the twentieth century still saw barricades constructed across Europe, but without ever regaining what had once given the device such a unique role, almost the same despite very varied circumstances, from the sixteenth to the nineteenth century – from the rebellion against Henri III, to the final week facing the troops of Adolphe Thiers.

The role of the barricade, as we have seen, was not limited to its strictly military aspect – a fact shown in purest form by the photographs of Spartakists firing from behind rolls of newsprint, or of Spanish militiamen sheltering to fire from behind a dead horse. Throughout the nineteenth century, the barricade was a *symbolic form of insurrection*: to unpave a street, overturn a cart, pile up furniture, is to give a signal, to show one's determination to fight, and fight together. Barricades form a network that links combatants together and lends unity to the struggle, even where it lacks a leader or overall plan.

It is the memory of this symbolic role that explains the strange idea that came over the students on the night of 10 May 1968. Raising barricades on the rue Gay-Lussac obviously did not signal a plan to overthrow the Gaullist regime by force. Instead, resorting to this archaic and glorious procedure made a link with the past in order to

Spartakist barricade in the press district of Berlin, January 1919

indicate in poetic fashion the students' determination to subvert the existing order.

The 'classic' barricade also functioned as a theatrical stage. From atop their paving-stones the insurgents harangued the soldiers, trying to convince them not to fire on their brothers. Sometimes they succeeded (the 5th and 53rd regiments of the line going over to the insurrection on 29 July 1830), sometimes not (the death of two women on the barricade at the Porte Saint-Denis on 23 June 1848). This risk of contamination explains the change of strategy by the forces of order, who after 1848 tried to avoid dividing their troops into small units, more susceptible to the eloquence of the barricade than large masses welded into anonymity.

Though the twentieth century had no shortage of riots, insurrections and revolutions, the barricade remained a marginal element. The reasons for this are material rather than psychological or

Barcelona, 19 July 1936

political. The physiognomy of cities has changed: under the axe of the demolishers, the old, narrow, winding streets inherited from the Middle Ages made way for boulevards and avenues whose width and straight lines are unpropitious for barricades. The rue Saint-Martin was easier to block than the boulevard Magenta: Haussmann knew this, and his disciples applied the same principle in the majority of large European cities. At the same time, the armies assembled by the state to deal with civil war have been modernized. In the face of an effective artillery, backed by tanks and other mechanical weapons, the barricade no longer pulls the same weight.

Finally, the way in which cities are peopled has also changed. The traditional barricade was erected in a street by its own inhabitants, men, women and children, who also worked there or close by, and were ready to die there. With the capitalist organization of urban life, this street-village has disappeared. Proletarians were compelled to work increasingly far from where they lived, and the site of struggle shifted to the factory, where it made no sense to pile up paving-stones.

All the same, if we accept that the barricade functioned above all as an *obstruction* to the forces of repression, we can still find modern equivalents – where such an obstruction affects no longer streets but instead rail and road communications, the flows of energy and information. Future insurrections will rediscover, without knowing it, without saying it, and without paving-stones, the way of acting by stifling the power of the state that made the good old barricade so effective.

Illustration Credits

Page 80: Barricades in Prague, June 1848. Source: Joseph Rudl, *Die Barrikaden Prag's in der verhängnißvollen Pfingstwoche 1848: Dargestellet in einigen Bildern mit beleuchtendem Texte aus den Begebenheiten dieser Täge* (Prague: Landau, 1848).

Page 97: (Top) Barricade on the rue Saint-Maur before the attack by the forces of General Lamoricière, Sunday, 25 June 1848. Daguerrotype by Thibault. © RMN-Grand Palais (musée d'Orsay). © Hervé Lewnandowski.

(Bottom) Barricade on the rue Saint-Maur after the attack by the forces of General Lamoricière, Monday, 26 June 1848. Daguerrotype by Thibault. © RMN-Grand Palais (musée d'Orsay). © Hervé Lewnandowski.

Page 117: Barricade on the rue d'Allemagne (now avenue Jean-Jaurès) at the crossroads with the rue de Sébastopol (now rue Lally-Tollendal), 1871. © BHVP/Roger-Viollet.

Page 124: Spartakist barricade in the press district of Berlin, January 1919. Anonymous photo.

Page 125: Barcelona, 19 July 1936. Photo by Agustí Centelles.

Index